ALSO BY NAOMI JUDD

Love Can Build a Bridge (autobiography)

Naomi's Home Companion

CHILDREN'S BOOKS

Love Can Build a Bridge (lyrics)

Guardian Angels

NAOMI'S
BREAKTHROUGH GUIDE

20 CHOICES TO TRANSFORM YOUR LIFE

Naomi Judd

Simon & Schuster

New York   London   Toronto   Sydney

Simon & Schuster
Rockefeller Center
1230 Avenue of the Americas
New York, NY 10020

SIMON & SCHUSTER and colophon are registered trademarks
of Simon & Schuster Inc.

For information regarding special discounts for bulk purchases,
please contact Simon & Schuster Special Sales at 1-800-456-6798
or business@simonandschuster.com.

Designed by Joel Avirom and Jason Snyder

Manufactured in the United States of America

10   9   8   7   6   5   4   3

Library of Congress Cataloging-in-Publication Data

Judd, Naomi.
    Naomi's breakthrough guide : 20 choices to transform your life / Naomi Judd.
        p. cm.
    1. Self-actualization (Psychology) 2. Judd, Naomi. I. Title.
    BF637.S4J84 2004
    158.1—dc22

                                                        2003059173

ISBN 0-7432-3662-9

to Jennie

So you taught me that a paradigm is how we look at and think about ourselves and all that is around us. It's the psychological framework we set for ourselves to operate within every day. A paradigm tells us our version of what is real and what isn't. It's how we're feeling about ourselves and our relationship to others. Little did I know as I lifted the latch of the white picket-fence gate on that dismal day in 1990 that you would be so instrumental in my paradigm shift.

Entering your magical garden for the first time, with its bird feeders, squirrel feeders, and the smell of fresh earth, I sensed this was a place where things and people could grow. When stepping-stones led to a unique cottage, you greeted me with open arms. Your welcome hug said, Well, come on in. I sank into the sofa and burrowed down into myself, Laddie on one side, Pip on the other. I am as comfy there as I am in my favorite flannel pj's.

Each time I visit you, I feel I'm coming home to myself and my best friend. You are the same age as my mother, yet you and I share the same birthday. Friendship is the most mature of all loves. I love it when you tell me those dumb jokes. I'm grateful when you hold my hand if I cry. I cherish it when you lead me in prayer. Your life of integrity and devotion to service has made you a champion, a facilitator, and a mentor to thousands. I've been privileged to know some outstanding women. You, though, next to my mother, Polly, are the most influential in my life. I love you very much.

I pray now that your compassion and wisdom will shine through in these pages to inspire a healthier paradigm shift in others too, as they have for me.

Contents

NAOMI'S
BREAKTHROUGH GUIDE

There's only one corner of the universe you can be certain of improving, and that's your own self. —ALDOUS HUXLEY

1 Peace of Mind Is the Goal

Welcome to a fantastic voyage of self-discovery! Fasten your seat belt, because we're going to explore the greatest frontier: our *inner* space. We're going to take a good look at ourselves, the only place where we have the power to change. We're going to focus on twenty breakthrough choices. These hard-won discoveries transformed my life for the better. I believe they can help you become happier too. Choice #1 is PEACE OF MIND IS THE GOAL. That's the destination of this journey of self-awareness.

If you know anything about me, you know that my life's taken a few unexpected curves and crashes along the way. But hey, at least I can say I took the scenic route! I'm living proof of the saying "That which doesn't kill us makes us stronger." But because of these experiences, I've discovered a lot about the body-mind-spirit connection. Understanding how these interact and impact health and happiness may surprise you.

You may know that in 1964, at age eighteen, back in the small town of Ashland, Kentucky, I missed my high school graduation to give birth to Wynonna. Then, in my twenties, I had an unhappy first marriage. It did, however, produce my darling Ashley. The inevitable divorce forced me to become a single, working mom struggling alone with my two girls. Without skills or an education, I was relegated to minimum-wage jobs, like clerk, receptionist, and waitress. I even had to resort to welfare and food stamps. It was desperate and demeaning. So I put myself through college in my thirties and got an RN degree.

In 1979, I took a giant risk chasing a preposterous dream. I arrived in Nashville in an old, beat-up car with two young, high-spirited girls in the backseat. At age thirty-seven, I turned Wy's and my preposterous fantasy of becoming recording artists into reality. In my forties and fifties, I've proven medical authorities wrong after they coldly handed me a death sentence because of hepatitis C.

Today I'm radiantly healthy and happier than ever, and I'm using my restored energy to help others learn about themselves. Folks like you frequently come up to me on the street, in restaurants and airports, or at the grocery checkout counter and ask: How in the world have I survived all my broken-heart attacks, whacks, and setbacks? You wonder how my husband, Larry, and I have managed to stay in love since 1979. You wonder how Wynonna and Ashley have both achieved phenomenal success as artists—and how in the world, despite everyone's hectic schedule, we maintain our all-important familial bond.

It has been unbelievably frustrating for me not to have the time or the place to respond with answers to these questions and concerns, which are so obviously important to you and me. I've learned so much about how easy it is to make smarter choices and achieve greater peace of mind. That's why I'm both relieved and excited to have finally written this book for you.

You know me only through the media, as I am now, so which is harder for you to imagine: (1) that I was once lonely, broke, aimless, and desperate, or (2) that you can discover your own latent talent, enjoy a happy marriage and family life, be financially secure, and even beat your disease?

I hope you will learn more about your potential as I share with you just how I did it. I'm going to explain how I learned to make the choices that allowed me not only to survive but to thrive—to be more happy, healthy, and content than I have ever been before. I've done it against great odds—and I'm confident you can too.

When I come to your neighborhood, I hope we can get together to discuss where the choices I describe in this book have led you emotionally, mentally, physically, and spiritually. Ideas get even stronger when shared.

I thank God for my handicaps, for through them
I've found myself, my work and my God. —HELEN KELLER

A Dead End Is Just a Good Place to Turn Around

As you sit there reading this page, how happy, peaceful, and fulfilled are you, on a scale of one to ten? Are you outside the door of the life you always thought you should have, desperately banging on it to get in? How about your relationships? Are you, as comedian Caroline Rhea put it, "one bad relationship from becoming one of those women who has thirty cats"? Is there some discrepancy between what you think you are worthy of and how other people are currently treating you? Is your job as satisfying as it can be? Do you get recognized and rewarded? Do you look forward to your day? Or do you feel like you're stuck in a rut? Are you able to handle any crisis, small or large, that broadsides you? Are you feeling lost, listless, restless, or bored? Are you battling an illness?

News flash: There's *so* much more out there waiting for you, my friend!

I define happiness as a state of well-being, full of the joy that comes from being satisfied with whatever you have and enjoying every day to the utmost. Health, happy marriage, good friends, well-rounded kids, financial security, comfortable lifestyle, and a purpose that allows you to express your talent and pay your bills—that's my definition of success. What's yours? One way to identify it is to ask yourself: If I won the lottery, what would I change in my life? What would I keep the same?

The concepts in this book will help you find your own unique path through the issues you're facing and make the choices that will bring greater satisfaction. Within these covers are questions to increase your awareness of the answers that are locked inside you. Hopefully you will come to understand just why you act and react the way you do—and why you aren't quite living the kind of life you'd like. You'll recognize people around you who are traveling the same path. You'll also begin spotting others in your life who are going off in completely different directions. You'll learn how to say to them, "Bless you as you go."

As we set out together, let me go on the record now and say that there is nothing different or special about Naomi Judd. I'm not an expert. An expert is just somebody from out of town with slides. I don't do slides or flowcharts. If anything, I've been an expert at making mistakes. I've lived out there on life's highways for twenty years as a touring entertainer. I am a "Road" scholar with a Ph.D. from the School of Hard Knocks. I majored in crisis management. This entire country's my research lab. You could say that I'm a student of human nature. I go wherever my questions lead. I'm always learning whatever I'm trying to teach.

I'll reveal some of my own personal mistakes and calamities to show you, by example, how a dead end is just a good place to turn around. I'll report cutting-edge research on health and the psychology of happiness. There's also commonsense wisdom I've absorbed over the years from everyday folks as I've traveled coast to coast. To quote Woodrow Wilson, "I not only use all the brains I have, but all I can borrow."

I'll be revealing stories of famous people throughout this book since I know them personally and you know about them. I'll give you a behind-the-scenes peek at how they've been able to evolve on their voyages of self-discovery. I'm convinced you'll see how much alike we all truly are. Also, I want to prove to you that no one's born with their destiny stamped on their forehead. Nobody's born a great anything. We make the choices to fulfill our destiny.

The lowest ebb is the turn in the tide.
—HENRY WADSWORTH LONGFELLOW

Crisis Means Danger and Opportunity

It has been a decade now since I wrote my candid autobiography, *Love Can Build a Bridge*. Since then, as difficult as these last ten years have been, I'm satisfied that every obstacle I've faced has been part of a much bigger plan. Suffering makes sense if you can step back and view it in a larger context. Everything in your life and mine is exactly the way it's supposed to be. This was a huge revelation for me! Discovering this lets me breathe a lot easier, gives me greater peace of mind, and allows me to expand instead of contract.

Stop now and give this insight time to register with you. Every crisis offers a treasure trove of information about ourselves. (That's why they call it an *emergency*—you *emerge* and *see*.) A crisis prompts us to raise our consciousness and choose to open up to more of who we're meant to be. It also shows us just how many more dimensions there are to living. In the Chinese language, the word "crisis" is made up of two characters, depicting "danger" and "opportunity." It's always up to you and me to choose, at every crossroads, which path we take.

Consider your latest crisis. What was the nature of the impending threat, and what was the potential opportunity? What path did you go down? Why? What did you learn? How will you react next time?

During my crisis with hepatitis C, I chose the opportunity route. I made the choice to tap into a reserve strength that was deeper than I ever expected. Call it resilience, will, or moral fiber. In the process, I discovered what it takes to persevere in the face of the loss of what I hold dearest—and to stare death squarely in the eye. If I hadn't chosen to go for the opportunities to learn from my predicament, I'd probably be dead. Surviving isn't as complicated or mysterious as you're probably thinking. What it takes is (1) a great deal of faith in oneself, (2) an openness to taking in new information, and (3) a belief in a higher power.

What we achieve inwardly will change outer reality. —OTTO RANK

Dare to Fulfill Your Birthright!

I was feeling terribly ill and, of course, mentally depressed when doctors announced there was no known cure for hepatitis C and I'd probably die within three years. The only available treatment was interferon, and my first round of interferon injections didn't have the desired effect. Instead of submitting to despair, I chose to step out in faith and trust in God. Hebrews 11:1 states, "Now faith is the substance of things hoped for, the evidence of things not seen." I promised God, myself, and my family that I was going to learn everything I could about this mysterious disease. I vowed to figure out a way to beat it. I also made the decision that I would eventually share whatever I learned, to somehow help others.

I was one angry patient when I experienced firsthand the grim reality of what's wrong with our health care system. (I refer to it as the "wealth care system.") I naively expected managed care to manage to care! Rather than asking how I was feeling physically, emotionally, mentally, or spiritually, the first question anyone asked was "Who's your insurance carrier?" Even though I'm a nurse, I was shocked. I'm now fully aware that our medical system needs healing. I want to be part of helping medicine treat the whole person and teach prevention and wellness.

You may not be facing a medical crisis. But whatever mental, emotional, physical, or spiritual challenges you are now facing, I'm offering information, hope, and comfort in these pages. I'm sentencing you to live.

If your ship doesn't come in, swim out to it. —JONATHAN WINTERS

You Are One—
Body, Mind, and Spirit

I had already begun studying everything I could get my hands on about hepatitis C, this "silent killer" that will kill four times more Americans than AIDS in the next decade. But it was journalist Bill Moyers's groundbreaking 1990 PBS documentary series *Healing and the Mind* that launched me into an investigation that wound up saving my life and expanding my consciousness. Bedridden, I watched one expert after another talk about different paths to healing. This was TV at its finest—"tell-a-vision." The award-winning Moyers special encouraged me to search for a different path to healing.

It was one of the most fascinating learning experiences of my adventurous life. As I delved into understanding how we are whole beings with emotions, lifestyles, and spiritual needs, I learned how our lifestyles can cause all sorts of mental distress and disease, and that good health is much more than the absence of disease. I was shocked to discover that 85 percent of all illnesses are stress related. In fact the World Health Organization has proclaimed stress to be the number-one global epidemic.

As a result of choosing to be proactive in fighting my disease, I had a physical breakthrough instead of a breakdown. It was a bitter, frightening battle, but I've won! In 1995, Dr. Bruce Bacon, a leading liver specialist and former medical adviser for the American Liver Foundation, pronounced the hepatitis C virus completely gone from my body. I represent the "body of evidence" of what I've learned.

This book represents another phase of my insatiable curiosity. I no longer consider myself to be simply an entertainer who's miraculously survived a life-threatening disease. I've graduated. I'm an "infotainer." I have always been a communicator—whether writing or singing a song, acting, giving a lecture, chatting with a stranger, or writing a book. I'm living proof that your choice of how to respond to a situation constitutes your ultimate power. It's time for you to find that power and begin getting all you deserve.

Each time we squarely face and successfully handle a problem, we become aware of even more options. My hope is that somewhere in these pages you'll recognize just how broad your range of choices is. Psychologist Abraham Maslow once said, "When all you have is a hammer, you see everything as a nail." In these upcoming pages, you're going to assemble your very own personalized toolbox full of emotional, physical, and spiritual tools. That way you can reach for them anytime you desire to fix something in your mind, body, or spirit.

When we stand together
It's our finest hour.
We can do anything
If we keep believing in the power.
—"Love Can Build a Bridge," Naomi Judd

Winning the Peace Prize

You don't have to be going through a hard time to benefit from the messages in this book. You might just have a yearning to become even happier. As your guide, I'll recommend that you slow down and turn down the volume of background noise in your life. Also, get ready for an epiphany as you come to understand how your self-esteem affects everything. We'll be working primarily on your relationship with yourself since it predicts the kind of relationships you'll have with others.

And if we win, we win the grand prize, the peace prize. That's because *peace of mind is the ultimate goal.* I've met kings and queens, world leaders, presidents, movie stars, rock stars, Nobel laureates, sports figures, and every other kind of famous personage. I can tell you we all want the same thing—peace of mind. That is why it is Choice #1.

Peace of mind isn't the absence of problems; peace of mind comes from your ability to deal with them. Peace of mind is both the first and the ultimate choice we make through exercising the other nineteen choices in this book. The more we understand ourselves and what's standing in the way of our being as happy and healthy as we can, and the more eager we become to risk following our dreams and offering our gifts to others, the more worthy we feel, the more we choose peace of mind.

This doesn't mean we will ever have all the answers. As humans, we are always in the process of becoming. But when we trust ourselves and the process, we evolve. Once Wy was lying in my lap on our couch in the kitchen crying about her divorce. "Mom, am I ever going to have it all together?" She was hoping to hear a soothing "Of course you will, sweetheart." Instead, I responded, "No, 'cause that would be like saying you could breathe, eat, or sleep once and for all. Life is a process. Let's stick together and do the best we can. We either find a way or make a way, one day at a time." There was a long pause. Wy sighed, "Yeah, 'cause if it ain't one thing, it's your mother."

Success is a journey, not a destination. The doing is usually more than the outcome. —ARTHUR ASHE

Life Is Short, but It's Wide

Today is the first day of the rest of an altogether more peaceful and fulfilling life. You can consciously choose a better way of relating to yourself and others. You can attract more of what you desire and discover brand-new opportunities.

We get only one go-around in life, so let's get it right! Don't waste another single drop of your potential for happiness. If you've been sleepwalking through parts of your life, this is your wake-up call. Open your eyes now to the truth all around you. Open your heart and mind to what really matters to you. Begin to ask questions. Begin to think and behave like the person you want to be! I know you can do it.

Select a spot that is quiet and comfortable for you, as my kitchen table is for me. Designate that space your own sacred "growth place." Pretend that I have just made you your favorite comfort meal, and picture me sitting in an empty chair as your companion and support.

Here we grow . . .

*Few is the number who think with their own minds
and feel with their own hearts.* —ALBERT EINSTEIN

2 Change Your Mind, Change Your World

My awareness of Choice #2—CHANGE YOUR MIND, CHANGE
YOUR WORLD—came when I was only seventeen. The
night before my senior year of high school, I was left alone in our
family home for the first time in my incredibly sheltered childhood. Mama and Daddy had taken my younger brother Brian,
who was just fifteen years old at the time, to Ohio, searching for
a miracle to cure his Hodgkin's disease. It was the worst thing
that had ever happened to any of us. I was emotionally devastated
by his suffering and incredibly scared about what was happening
to our whole family. That night, an older boy I'd been dating came
by my house while my parents were gone, and I had sex for the
first time. Unprotected. I had been the good girl in our Andy Grif-
fith, Mayberry kind of town, and two months later, I realized I
was pregnant. Oops! It was my first personal catastrophic event.

*Many men owe the grandeur of their lives to their
tremendous difficulties.* —CHARLES SPURGEON

Daze of Our Lives

As I watched JFK's funeral procession on our black-and-white TV that cold, dreary November day in 1963, it was a sign to do something about my own drama. I trudged up to my bedroom and broke open my pink poodle piggy bank. I took my $1.50 allowance, called a cab (I couldn't drive), and went to see our family doctor after office hours. Dr. Wayne Franz thought I had come there to ask about Brian's disease. It took a while to work up my nerve and sputter out my shameful question: "Doctor, is it biologically possible to get pregnant the first time you have sex?" The kind man who'd taken care of me since infancy lowered his head and began to weep. He didn't have any answers—not about Brian, who was dying a hideous death, and now not for me.

That moment changed my life forever. In the silence that followed, I realized that change is the true nature of the universe. But I didn't want things to change! I loved my life just as it was. I was a very sheltered seventeen-year-old and nowhere near ready to be thrust into marriage and motherhood. But what I came to see is that change often happens when you least expect it and when it's most inconvenient. As in an accident, you don't even realize what's happening until it's happening. But you have to deal with it anyway.

Whenever any crisis hits, whether it is personal, like what was happening to me, or universal, like the tragedy of September 11, it either brings people together or rips them apart. My beloved brother would eventually succumb to his illness, and my parents' marriage would then disintegrate. I saw firsthand why 85 percent of marriages end in divorce following the death of a child.

If you love everything you will perceive the divine mystery in things. Once you perceive it, you will begin to comprehend it better every day. And you will come to love the whole world with an all-embracing love. —FYODOR DOSTOYEVSKY

Born to Win

Most people can't know or don't take time to contemplate all the ramifications of a major change. It just happens. The saving grace, though, is that you and I always get to decide what meaning we attach to every change, good or bad, that happens to us. How we apply the lessons we learn from each experience to helping us face the rest of our life is up to us. That's why I've subtitled this book *20 Choices to Transform Your Life*. The ways we choose to react to whatever happens to us can transform us. It's all part of a grand design. That doesn't mean we can know, when it's happening, what that design is. Often the only thing we can do is hang on tight and trust we'll see the meaning later.

When I look at my life in this way, I understand that those teenage events transformed me—I became independent and self-reliant at an early age. My unexpected pregnancy, Brian's death, and my parents' conflicts forced me to realize that the only security I would ever have in this world would have to come from within myself. Until these tragedies struck my family, I had the most secure home life imaginable. Then the experience of losing all I relied on, all at once, showed me security is just an illusion.

Just like me, you can never count on the outside world to stay the way you want. Yours and my only real security lies in realizing that the deepest source of our identity comes from God. As children of the supreme Creator of the universe, *we're born to win!* When you're confident about this connection, then you are secure within. You can stay centered no matter what's unraveling around you. You find assurance and comfort that you're never alone. You have a sense of confidence that you're equipped to face any reality boldly.

All of life's challenges offer us an opportunity to grow, if we see them through spiritual eyes and use them in this way. My brother Mark turned to his faith to deal with the grief of Brian's death and our parents' divorce. He's now a pastor. Brian's best friend, Jimmy Lett, was so devastated by his death that Jimmy became a doctor. I eventually became an RN.

We're all driven by the winds of change.
Seems like nothing ever stays the same.
It's faith that guides me around the bend.
Life's forever beginning, beginning again.
Flow on, "River of Time."
—"River of Time," Naomi Judd, written for Brian

The Deeper Meaning

I call my mentor Dr. Rachel Naomi Remen a "wounded healer" because although she suffers from Crohn's disease, a lifelong, chronic illness, she dedicates her life to helping others heal. Rachel taught me to start seeing the sacred meaning in everything that happens to us. When I got pregnant at age seventeen, not only did I find the source of my inner strength, but also I was blessed with one of the best things that's ever happened to me: Wynonna Ellen Judd was born!

Any type of catastrophic event makes us take stock of our life, find the message, and change for the better. My girlfriend Jacqui is a great example. Jacqui is an attractive forty-three-year-old who's worked hard all her life to become general manager of Cox Cable in Baton Rouge. On the morning of 9/11 she was in an important meeting in the executive boardroom. Suddenly a secretary rushed in with the shocking announcement that the Twin Towers had been struck. In a flash, everyone scrambled to call home. Jacqui sat there alone at the empty table littered with purses, briefcases, pads, pencils, and coffee mugs. She had no one to call. She went straight home, but still there were no phone messages from anyone checking on her. The lack of messages was a message.

Jacqui grew up in a foster home and had fought hard to break the corporate glass ceiling. But on the night of 9/11, she realized her life was not complete. Rather than being stuck in victimhood, she chose to use this lesson to transform her life. She has since adopted two beautiful babies, April and Bree, and is sending her niece to college.

The horror of the murderous terrorist attacks on 9/11 proved to us all that change happens whether we want it or not. It stripped us down and made each of us reassess and acknowledge what matters most. We got back in touch with our feelings and opened our hearts. We began looking for a better way to think and be. We see from the stories of bravery and resilience that as humans we need to make sense of tragedy.

Nobody uses the disadvantages of her life to better advantage than my friend Dolly Parton. She's turned tragedy into triumph by singing of the extremes of her rural childhood in the Smoky Mountains of Sevierville, Tennessee. Dolly's mother, Avie Lee, had to use rags to sew her a coat for school. Yet Dolly sings the praises of a mother's love as she describes the warmth of her "Coat of Many Colors." Be like Dolly, who's one of the smartest women I know. Use what's happened to you rather than letting it use you.

Nothing in life is to be feared. It is only to be understood.
—MARIE CURIE

When You Change Your Mind, You Change Your World

As soon as we give ourselves the power to seek meaning in a challenge, we also give ourselves the power to change. Every expert I spoke to, whether a doctor, behavioral scientist, molecular biologist, physicist, or biochemist, agreed on one thing: nothing can get better in our lives until we decide to change the way we're thinking about a problem. I've always liked Rita Mae Brown's definition: "Insanity is doing something over and over again, but expecting different results." To get different results, we first have to change our thinking.

It's actually the significance that you and I attach to our experiences, and then the way we choose to incorporate the lessons into our future, that makes us either more fulfilled or worse off than before. When I began to understand this, everything began improving in my life. I say to myself all the time now: "Wait a minute, I know there's another way of looking at this." Changing my mind has changed my life!

One of my friends is Dr. Christiane Northrup, a respected ob-gyn and best-selling author of *Women's Bodies, Women's Wisdom* and *The Wisdom of Menopause*. One night over supper in Chris's village of Yarmouth, Maine, we discussed the terrible fact that in this country a woman is beaten by her husband or live-in lover every nine to thirteen seconds. Yet, even in these violent circumstances, said Chris, "change is possible as soon as a woman chooses to see why it's happening. No matter what's happened in the past in her life, a woman always has the power to change what an experience means to her, and thus, change her experience emotionally, physically, and spiritually. Therein lies the potential for her healing."

Enlightenment is the moment of truth, the sudden emergence of new insight in an act of intuition. —ARTHUR KOESTLER

Your Turn Now

You too can begin to make sense of your troubles by changing how you are thinking about them.

- What was your first big milestone, challenge, or crisis?

- Looking back, what impressions did it make? What did you learn from that event? What characteristic traits did it bring out in you?

- How did it affect others around you? What did they learn from the same event?

- What is a challenge you are facing now?

- What could be right about what's wrong? What opportunity is there in the danger?

- If you were outside your life observing, what would you think of how you are handling this situation? What would you change?

- Expand how you are thinking about this problem by exploring all the possible ways it could turn out, no matter how implausible.

Nothing outside yourself can save you. Nothing outside yourself can give you peace. —A Course in Miracles

3 Life Is a Series of Multiple-Choice Questions

*E*piphanies are sudden, intuitive perceptions or insights. I've come to recognize them as symbolic revelations from God. I was twenty-two and living off Sunset Strip in Hollywood when I was struck with one. I'd had a worthless boyfriend whom I'd broken up with. In retribution, the low-life scum broke into my house one night and beat me in a jealous rage. After he shot up heroin (I'd had no idea he did drugs), he passed out. At 3 A.M., I escaped to the West Hollywood sheriff's station to file assault and breaking-and-entering charges and get a restraining order. The deputy informed me the guy was an ex-con and warned me to stay somewhere else while they went to arrest him.

As always during that time of my life, I had no money, but the sympathetic night clerk at a motel down the street felt sorry for me and my two sleepy girls and gave us a room. I was looking in the mirror on the bathroom medicine cabinet, trying to cover my black eye with makeup. There was nothing I could do to hide my swollen, busted lip. Suddenly I had an epiphany. It dawned on me that my life was as messed up as that battered face staring back at me!

A psycho had broken my China Doll façade, and I was automatically programmed to start covering it up with makeup. But rather than just superficially covering up my face (and my life) again, I began facing the deeper issue of who I'd become. In that fateful moment, I dug beneath the superficial reflection and began to honestly look within. In that moment, I promised myself, "No more masks." Just as my cuts and bruises would begin healing from the inside out, so could I.

Just one great idea can completely revolutionize your life.
—EARL NIGHTINGALE

Use Some Windex on the Window to Your Soul

This heavy story is where I get my phrase "looking in the Mirror of Truth." At the time, living off Sunset Strip, in my twenties, raising the girls alone, I felt trapped and overwhelmed by my dire physical circumstances. No money, no education, no contacts, no emotional support. I was not aware that old, unresolved trauma—from my pregnancy, from Brian's death, and from my parents' divorce—was clouding my judgment and making me feel crummy about myself.

But as I looked into that mirror, I began to question how in tarnation I'd gotten into this scary predicament. An answer hurled to the surface of my consciousness: *I'd done it all to myself!* Day by day, through the years, I'd kept choosing this dead-end path. My desperate situation that night was a culmination of all the small and large inappropriate choices I'd been making. In a flash, I had a profound breakthrough—Choice #3: LIFE IS A SERIES OF MULTIPLE-CHOICE QUESTIONS. I saw clearly that it is through our choices that our lives take shape.

That scary night at the hands of someone whose own bad choices had escalated into his becoming dangerously violent divided us once and for all. He had a breakdown. I chose to have a breakthrough. I'd lost sight of the truth that belief in God meant I deserved better. I was worthy of attracting better people. But in order for that to happen, I needed to begin to choose differently, right then and there!

Psychiatrist and best-selling author Dr. M. Scott Peck writes about this in his incredible book *The Road Less Traveled*. He says that "sooner or later, if people are to be healed, they must learn that the entirety of one's adult life is a series of personal choices. If they can accept this totally, then they become free. To the extent that they cannot accept this, they will forever feel themselves victims." Our liberation, our healing, comes from the admission that our predicament is actually a result of all the choices we've made. No one's done it to us. We've actually been doing it to ourselves all along. Ouch! People are treating us the way we've trained them to treat us.

This awareness brings us to a choice right now. No matter how trapped you or I might be feeling in any given moment, we can still choose a different reaction to our circumstances.

No one exemplifies this truth more than Holocaust survivor Viktor Frankl. Despite all the humiliations and emotional and physical traumas of life in a concentration camp, Viktor maintained his dignity and chose to remain focused on surviving. "One thing no one can ever take from me is my freedom to choose," he wrote later in his powerful book *Man's Search for Meaning*. It was Viktor's awareness of his power to choose that helped him to survive in a tragedy when millions perished.

Like Viktor Frankl, you and I always get to choose our reaction to whatever's going on around us. This is the power that will set us free.

Cocreators with God

In that moment of truth in front of the mirror, I saw that I was
more than a battered face; my life had a greater meaning than
the choices I'd been making up to that point. I began to see that
choices are sacred. God created us and gives us the opportunities
to make choices. This means that we can become cocreators with
God in deciding our future.

I didn't fully realize it then, but I've since come to understand
that there is an invisible, spiritual world. As we make inspired,
conscious choices, we're opening up to infinite possibilities.

There was another Mirror of Truth the night of my beating.
Behind the front desk at the sheriff's station where I went to seek
help was a two-way mirror. I could see only myself, but on the
other side was an invisible source of help and support. I found
this out only a few weeks later when I took Wy's Brownie troop
on a field trip to the station.

So is it true with God. He is always there, invisible but all-
knowing and available for us to turn to.

*In order for our suffering to have any meaning at all, it must
ultimately increase the capacity of all humankind both to love
and be loved.*—JOAN BORYSENKO, PH.D.

Figuring Out What We Don't Want Helps Us Make Better Choices

When it comes time to make a choice, realizing what we don't want can help us see what we do want to do. That epiphany in front of the motel mirror caused me to look back with newly informed eyes at my choices up till then. I immediately became clear about what I didn't want anymore. I didn't like the discrepancy between the way I'd been raised and the way Wy and Ashley were now growing up. I no longer wanted any part of the overstimulated, materialistic, phony Hollywood lifestyle. What was important to me was Wy and Ash knowing their heritage and being close to our family. I also wanted more time and opportunity to tune in to them.

Once I became aware of the huge discrepancy between the choices I'd been making and my true values, I began the necessary steps toward bringing my life into alignment with my values.

All I did was carve away everything that wasn't David.
—MICHELANGELO, ON HOW HE MADE A BLOCK OF MARBLE INTO THE MASTERPIECE STATUE

Baggage Claim

Although we always have choices, we often operate on automatic pilot. We're bogged down by emotional baggage from the past. But as soon as we choose to claim our "stuff," we unpack and discard unhealthy burdens. Abuse of any kind is a learned behavior. Hitting, shouting, severe punishments, and verbal and physical abuse can cause emotional baggage. When we were children, our impressionable minds perceived abuse as somehow justified by our unlovableness. Rather than understanding that it was the response of adults who had been treated this way themselves as children—and that it didn't occur because *we* were bad—we accepted this behavior. We became emotionally damaged and began to not love ourselves. Often, as adults, unless we have learned that the abuse wasn't our fault, we repeat this vicious cycle.

As I faced myself in the Mirror of Truth that night, I also began to look at my abuser. I saw how he was living out his family curse—he had been beaten as a child and had run away from his own unsafe home at age fourteen. This psychological awareness as well as my decision to accept responsibility for my predicament allowed my feelings toward him to shift. As a consequence, I was able to forgive him and leave the experience behind.

If you were abused as a child, chances are the person who attacked you, like my attacker, had also been abused as a child. A little boy who sees his dad hurt his mom is four times more likely to become an abuser himself. As many as 81 percent of men and women in mental hospitals have experienced physical or sexual abuse. Over 50 percent of prostitutes were incest victims or molested as children. Women who are sexually abused as girls are 2.4 times more likely to be victimized as women. Since they have no sense of self-worth, they have no emotional or physical boundaries. They don't ever get a chance to proceed though the normal steps of emotional development. Early in childhood, they feel labeled as worthless and trapped as sex objects. They're likely to medicate their emotional pain with mind-numbing drugs as a buffer against feelings that are simply too painful to bear.

Our deliverance from any terrible trauma and from resulting problems and addictions comes through choosing to be consciously awake. Deliverance comes from understanding that we may not have had much choice as children, but that as aware adults, we are free to choose to break the cycle. Whatever you may have suffered in your life, I know you're reading this book because you want to get better. I'm writing it because I have been healed and know you can be!

While we're growing up, it's as if we're just a passenger in a car being driven by someone else. We have no control. Now that we're older, we have license to drive ourselves. This puts us in the proverbial driver's seat. Instead of being blindly driven by our past, we can now take hold of the wheel, choose our direction, and steer boldly into our future.

Last year, at age seventy-four, my mom shocked everyone by getting a canary yellow BMW convertible. I exclaimed, "Mom, are you going through a second childhood?" She smiled as she responded, "Nope, I never had my first one. I'm proving to myself that it's never too late, though." *You go, girl!* Makes me think of a lyric in a song I wrote called "Cadillac Red": "She's washed and polished and full of high octane, cruising with the top down in the fast lane." It's never too late to have a happy childhood.

The one doctrine of my mother's teaching which was branded upon my senses was that I should never let anyone abuse me. "I'll kill you, gal, if you don't stand up for yourself," she would say. "Fight and if you can't fight, kick; if you can't kick, then bite."
—CORNELIA, BORN INTO SLAVERY IN TENNESSEE, 1844

Choose from the Following: (A) Victim, (B) Volunteer, or (C) Victor

Nowadays, when I speak at battered women's shelters, I gently introduce the concept of staring squarely into the Mirror of Truth. I encourage these women to start on the practice of looking back with informed eyes to discover the choices that have gotten them into abusive relationships. I try to help them see that the conflict between themselves and their partner is just a reflection of the conflict going on within them. We focus on their core issues, not the behavior of their partner. I suggest they look for any similarities between the situation they are in now and their past relationships. Hopefully they'll come to see exactly how things happened and that they deserve better. I promise them, "You'll see it when you believe it." I instruct them, "You're allowed to be a victim only once. After that you're considered a volunteer." Making better choices can make you a victor.

Every abusive relationship is potentially fatal.
—BRENDA, SERVING LIFE FOR MURDERING HER
ABUSIVE LOVER WHEN SHE FEARED FOR HER LIFE

When Bad Stuff Happens to Good People

If something bad happens in your life, it doesn't mean you're bad. It may just mean that, like me, you've made some poor choices. And likewise, if someone else does something bad to you, that doesn't necessarily mean he or she is all bad. It may just mean that he or she, too, made some poor choices. Poor choice making may come from experiences we had as children that we are repeating now. However, that does not relieve us from any of the responsibility. Every adult is responsible for the choices he or she makes. Accepting this responsibility is one of the first steps toward claiming greater happiness.

Let's make a clear distinction here between *accepting responsibility for a mistake* and *guilt*. Taking full responsibility for our actions engages our conscience by providing feedback about the negative consequences of poor choices. This involves telling ourselves the truth about the harmful effects of those choices not only on ourselves, but on others as well. Guilt just makes you feel crummy about yourself in general. Owning up to mistakes leads to healthy change; guilt leads to defensiveness, competition, rigidity, or hypersensitivity to criticism.

When I met Joan Borysenko, Ph.D., she explained that guilt is analogous to an autoimmune disease of the soul. Autoimmune disease occurs when the body attacks itself. Guilt can cause us to literally reject our own worth as human beings. It's an infliction that robs us of joy and can send us into a mode of self-protection. In her book *Guilt Is the Teacher, Love Is the Lesson,* Joan says that guilt can result in a person's organizing his or her life around the need to avoid fear rather than a desire to share love. When we allow ourselves to be pulled backward by negative emotions like fear, doubt, and guilt, we get into unhealthy behaviors like overachievement, perfectionism, lack of assertiveness, narcissism, and co-dependency.

William James, scientist and doctor, who fathered American psychology in the early 1900s, coined the term "soul sickness" to describe a syndrome of unhealthy guilt, chronic stress, perfectionism, and associated physical symptoms. James's body of work emphasized our need for spiritual conversion. Like James, I believe every one of our problems is based in a spiritual disconnection. Therefore they all also have a spiritual solution. We must meditate on what we believe about right and wrong and reconsider our place within the universe. Returning to a happy state is called "healthy-mindedness." Healthy-mindedness brings us back into alignment with our soul's deepest purpose and connection to God.

When I saw my beat-up face in the Mirror of Truth, I chose to take responsibility for my choices that had led to that moment. I didn't add to the beating by beating myself up. If I had succumbed to guilt, it would have been even harder to change—I wouldn't have trusted myself. But when I declared myself a winner because God loved me, I accepted the gift of being free to choose more wisely the next time.

One evening not so long ago, I was in between Ashley and Wy in a white stretch limousine. We were all dolled up in fancy gowns, on the way to the Oscars. As I looked out the limo window, we drove right by that Hollywood motel where my life changed so many years ago. With my two wonderful, successful adult daughters by my side, I reviewed the choices, made since that fateful night, that had led us to this better life.

Anyone who goes to a psychiatrist should have their head examined.
—SAMUEL GOLDWYN

Your Turn Now

How many more bad choices are you willing to make before you get around to looking into the Mirror of Truth? Wy, Ash, and I have a saying for this, based on a joke. A blonde phones 911 to report her house is on fire. Needing directions, the dispatcher asks, "How do we get there?" Ignoring the obvious, the dumb blonde responds, "Duh, big red truck!" If something we've been missing finally dawns on one of the three of us, we call it a "Duh, big red truck" moment. When I learned I was free to make better choices and change my circumstances, I immediately started attracting a better class of people. No more jealous, abusive, drugged ex-cons. Whew! Here's your hat, what's your hurry?

- Where are you in your most important relationships? Are you repeating an unhealthy pattern you were subjected to in childhood?

- What are the choices you've made in your life that have led you to where you are right now?

- On what belief systems have you been making choices? We are all making choices based on some value system. Are yours in line with your values?

If you're having trouble seeing how you make choices, try this exercise:

Take a very large piece of paper. Begin with the first *choice you made on your own—leaving home, perhaps, or going to college, or getting married. Write it down on a line like a branch of a tree.*

At the base of that branch, write down the choice
you didn't make *at that moment—staying single, staying
at home, whatever choice you didn't make.*

*Then from the choice you did make, draw a new line
that represents the next choice you made, and the choice
you didn't make from that one, and so on, till you have a
tree of your life's choices that looks like this:*

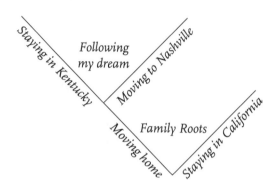

*Don't worry about putting down every choice, just
the ones that seem big. (However, don't make the mistake
of one woman, who complained about her husband
dragging her around the world and said she'd had no
choice about it. In fact, before each move, she did
choose—to go with him rather than break up or issue an
ultimatum. We always have choices, no matter our
circumstances.)*

*After you've got your major life choices on the tree, go
back and put the* value *represented by your choice in
the notch of each one. (On my tree would be "Move back
home to Kentucky in my twenties with Wy and Ashley"
versus "Stay in L.A." The value represented by my choice*

was "Family.") When you've put a value next to each choice, take a separate piece of paper and write down in a list all the values that you have used to make choices. If some are repeats—I would have "Family" several times—list them each time.

Now look at the list. What does it say about what matters to you and how you choose? If you don't like what you see, remember, you are free to choose differently now.

An affirmation to say out loud to yourself in the mirror:

I'm responsible for my unhappiness because of choices I've made. I can love myself more now and make better choices. My eyes are open to understanding that I deserve so much better. I'm ready to generate better choices. I am more together now, so I'll draw more together people and circumstances into my life.

When I was a child, I spoke as a child, I understood as a child, I thought as a child; but when I became a man I put away childish things. —1 CORINTHIANS 13:11

4 You Can Reverse Any Curse

*I*t was right after the beating. I was depressed and anxious about always being one paycheck away from the streets. I felt cursed by a constant sense of desperation. I just knew something had to change. I was in so much mental anguish that I was willing to do almost anything to start feeling better about myself.

I decided to learn from my mistakes by questioning how I'd gotten into such a fix. I'd read in a self-help book that a well-posed question is a question half answered. The more clearly I worded my questions, the more illuminated my path became. I began to see options and solutions. That's when Choice #4 dawned on me: YOU CAN REVERSE ANY CURSE. I had the power to stop the downward spiral. That realization was my next breakthrough to better health, happiness, and success.

To reverse the curse of my mistake-riddled past, I began with questioning just how I had gotten into this predicament in the first place. Then I kept refining the questions. How could I live beyond hand to mouth? What could I do to get some form of education or training to raise my standard of living?

No one in my family had worked in health care. I didn't even know a nurse. Yet I realized I had always been drawn toward helping others. I soon realized that, as it says in Matthew 6:21, "where your treasure is, there will your heart be also." It became very clear to me that my children and my desire to alleviate suffering in others were my priorities. Nursing appeared the next right step.

It hadn't been my idea to go to Hollywood; I went because of my then husband's job. Why couldn't I leave? It dawned on me that I could reverse the curse of living in Hollywood by returning to the happy part of my past—the rural life of Kentucky. I called the Kentucky Board of Nursing and asked questions about which college in the state had the highest rating. The answer was Eastern Kentucky University. So that's where I went.

My head was spinning with questions I'd never thought to ask before. What job could I do to put myself through college? I needed to be in classes during the day. Evenings I cared for Wy and Ash, but I could waitress after putting them to bed. It was a grueling, hard time, waitressing until 1 A.M., getting up to go to class, taking care of the kids. What kept me going on this path was that I immediately started feeling better. As I opened up to discovering more about myself, mistakes became less frequent.

Experience is what you get when you don't get what you wanted. It's been my experience that if I learn something from a failure, then it really wasn't a mistake after all. (Hey now, if you make that same mistake twice, is it déjà boo-boo?)

Mistakes are part of our evolution into maturity; let's remember to always learn something from them! It's not what happens to us, it's what we do with it that counts. My pal George Lucas, creator and director of *Star Wars,* shared with me how his own early struggles trying to get funding for his first movies and then digging out from their subsequent flops had prepared him for his eventual megasuccess. He says, "It's OK to lose; just don't lose the lesson."

Don't get me wrong. I'll welcome success over failure anytime I can get it. We all love getting that pat on the back. But when we screw up, it's a ripe opportunity to understand what caused our mistake so that we can do something different the next go-round. When Olympic gold-medal skater Scott Hamilton was asked what the most difficult jump is, I understood his answer: "The one you have to do right after you've fallen." No matter what the circumstances of our lives, we all have the power to reverse the curse.

The bravest sight in the world is to see a man struggling against adversity. —SENECA

Against All Odds

One of my very special friends is as comfortable floating in zero gravity, somewhere in outer space, as he is walking around on solid ground here on earth. This guy is living proof that you and I can choose to reverse the curse. Story Musgrave has been called the Dean of Astronauts. Yep, that's his real name, and what a story Story has! He spent a lot of mighty rough years getting prepared for his mission in life and in space. Story's great-grandfather, grandfather, both parents, and brother all committed suicide. The family's terrible mental illness, alcoholism, and abuse prevented him from graduating from high school.

But because Story chose to reverse his curse, his story turned out differently from that of the rest of his family. Despite his past, he chose to take responsibility for his future, open his mind, and explore new possibilities. The first thing he did was join the military to get a GED. He then earned a degree in mathematics and statistics. The next year, he received a master's in business administration, operational analysis, and computer programming. Next came a B.A. degree in chemistry and an M.D., followed by a master's in biophysics and physiology. Finally, a master's in literature. Last time we spoke, he was working on degrees in psychology and history. By my count, that's eight degrees! The guy has more degrees than a thermometer!

Whether Story was wearing scrubs operating in a hospital or in a space suit repairing the Hubble Space Telescope while circling planet Earth, he's relied on his strong survival instinct. So can you.

If you ask Story how in the world he's managed to keep his sanity, let alone accomplish so much, this is exactly what he'll tell you: "When you come into a world that all around you is far from perfect, you realize you are not the problem. You realize you need to survive the problem or distance yourself from it, or find another anchor. There are a lot of people who may be immersed in things that are not good, and you know that they blame themselves for it, or they somehow think they're part of it, or they've caused it, so they get wrapped up in it. They do not understand that some things are beyond their control, and they really need to use *themselves* as the anchor, and not the external world. Somehow, as far back as I can remember, even at the age of three, I thought, 'My goodness, what a world I have come into!' I looked at it from afar, and said, 'This ain't so good.' "

Another overcomer who teaches how to reverse the curse is Louise Hay. A best-selling author and speaker, she's a superstar in the world of healing. A child of the Depression, Louise was sexually abused at age five and subjected to extreme misery and poverty. But, like Story, she was determined to overcome her circumstances. She's an expert on how not to let your past control your future. Louise became self-reliant and entered the healing profession.

When it comes to teaching others what you need to learn for yourself, Louise literally wrote the book—*You Can Heal Your Life,* which I highly recommend. Louise continues to reinforce what she's learned by writing and speaking about healing.

Maybe, as Story puts it, "you didn't have it so good either." But Story, Louise, and I, and so many others I believe you can identify with, are now here to encourage you to achieve what you may have previously thought impossible. Louise Hay and Story Musgrave, like some of my other friends, had hideous childhoods, but they were able to step out of their circumstances and reverse the curse.

What we need are more people who specialize in the impossible.
—THEODORE ROETHKE

Make the Pain Go Away

As an RN, I administered lots of pain medications. So if you are in emotional or mental pain right now, I actually have good news for you. Story, Louise, and I can assure you personally that being discontented is actually a prerequisite for creating positive change. The three of us came to a point where we were so uncomfortable with the way things were that we were willing to do just about anything to make it better.

Are you at that point as well? Can you allow yourself to believe you are more than your past? Are you ready to do something constructive? In the hospital I recognized pain as the body's voice crying out for my patient to acknowledge that something's wrong.

If you're sitting in the middle of the freeway and you keep getting run over, it would be wise to get up and move. You certainly can't expect the traffic to stop. At some point we all need to grow up and realize this. Maturity involves getting up the courage to make change. As John Wayne put it, "Courage is being afraid but saddling up anyway." Being scared is what comes before courage. If you're in pain or scared right now, take comfort in the assurance that it's truly all part of the growing process.

I can personally tell you that it takes courage to start making life-altering changes. Some people would rather stay in a bad or negative situation because they haven't evolved enough to find the courage to change. In an unhealthy way, they choose the status quo—even though it makes them miserable—because it is familiar.

I was scared before I worked up the courage to go back to school in order to provide for my family. I knew that as a single mom raising two little girls I'd have to go through hell to work at night to support us and go to college during the day. But I earned much more than an RN degree in the process. I earned self-respect! Self-respect is the greatest feeling a human can experience. Where's your level of self-respect right now? If it's not high, what's it going to take to make you feel more proud of yourself?

Man needs difficulties; they are necessary for health.
—CARL JUNG

HOPE: Healing Of Painful Experiences

If you're having a hard time and are at the end of your rope, there's one other thing you can do—tie a knot and hang on. Hope will help you get you through. Hope helps you cope. The pain you may be experiencing is certainly real, but it can be temporary if you choose to use it as the motivation for your *healing of painful experiences.*

There have been so many scary times when hope was really all I had. Through the years, when I was broke or troubled by relationship problems, hope was the gift I could always give myself to keep from sinking further down in my fears. Hope was my constant companion during what I call my "dark night of the soul," the time when I was ill. The last word I spoke onstage every night in each city of my Farewell Tour was "hope." After singing "Love Can Build a Bridge," I left the stage with this self-fulfilling prophecy.

I believe in the power of love
And I believe there is always HOPE.
—"LOVE CAN BUILD A BRIDGE," NAOMI JUDD

Begin with the Elephant

I've finally figured out that any chance you or I have to reverse the curse and change for the better must originate with us. No one can do it for us. And we can't do it for anyone else either.

Here's how I realized this basic fact. I was worried about someone I love and went down to our lake one evening to pray. Absentmindedly tossing rocks into the water, I eventually noticed the ripple effect. I'd started an action that was directly influencing a reaction. It was a sign, a symbol. It slowly began to dawn on me that although I wasn't making any headway trying to change my loved one, maybe if I changed my reaction, it might have a ripple effect on that person.

There's an old saying: "It's a lot easier to spot the flea on someone else's shoulder than to see the elephant on your own." For many years I'd almost driven myself crazy trying to change Wy, Ash, and Larry into the people I felt they could be. My excuse was that I love them so much and believe in them, I just wanted them to become all they were capable of. I wanted them to be happy. Finally I faced up to the deeper truth: there's only one person I'll ever be able to change—myself! Interestingly enough, though, the positive changes you and I have the courage to make in ourselves will affect those around us.

Hepatitis C really forced me to concentrate on getting rid of my elephant. Not only have I made some positive changes, but lo and behold, they are still having a ripple effect on my entire family. That's why, if you'd like to help someone else, I strongly suggest you focus on setting an example.

You must be the change you want to see in the world.
—MAHATMA GANDHI

Malignant Memories

In talking about reversing the curse, I'm really concerned about people who have been severely traumatized. Because all their boundaries have been violated, they're usually unable to maintain any sense of significant self-worth or self-control. I have two girl-friends who were raped, and not long after the attacks they gained excess weight to "protect" themselves from perceived advances. They are still having trouble finding balanced relationships.

If you've suffered from physical, sexual, or emotional trauma, you are likely to have mood and anxiety problems. If unchecked, these can develop further into a myriad of self-destructive behaviors: self-mutilation, eating disorders (anorexia nervosa, bulimia, obesity), and addictions of all kinds, including substance abuse, multiple personality disorder and disassociation, nightmares, and flashbacks, just to name a few possibilities.

There are all sorts of resources available to help you heal from your wounds. One is *cognitive behavioral therapy*. "Cognitive" is about thinking, figuring out what's driving your emotions. "Behavioral" has to do with appropriate actions you choose based on this information. In cognitive behavioral therapy, you can find relief from depression, anxiety, and their related disorders. By focusing on unresolved anxiety, like a transition in a relationship and the communication issues it involves, you come to see exactly how your inappropriate emotions and beliefs have been fueling the problem behavior.

Sometimes medicines or other body therapies may be recommended as well. But there's never a replacement for digging deeply, asking questions, and then talking it out. Talk therapy rewires your brain for emotional literacy. It can actually stimulate your brain to produce those satisfying neurochemicals. For instance, if it's weight management you are struggling with, your doctor may recommend antidepressants or appetite suppressants to give you a more level playing field while you're dealing with the issue. But it's still imperative to allow all your emotions to come out in the open to be resolved.

Another approach I can personally recommend is EMDR, or *eye movement desensitization and reprocessing.* It's a well-researched method to help survivors of emotional trauma. It was first used on war veterans suffering from post-traumatic stress disorder (PTSD), and more recently on victims from the Oklahoma City bombing. It lessens distress from nightmares, flashbacks, insomnia, anxiety, and depression associated with PTSD.

If you have had emotional, physical, or sexual trauma, I strongly suggest you get professional help. Therapy has helped me tremendously at various times in my life. If you need it, I encourage you to raise up your hand and ask for help.

Theologian and author Wayne Mueller has been a therapist specializing in childhood traumas for almost thirty years. When I met with him, Wayne said, "Sometimes the worst things that happen to us can eventually turn out to be something that blesses not only us, but others." It's encouraging to know that if you work at it you can get to a point where you bless your past, not curse it.

If you or someone you know has been abused, check out Wayne's book *Legacy of the Heart: The Spiritual Advantage of a Painful Childhood.* It's full of inspiring stories of runaway teens, drug addicts, New York gang members, people with AIDS, and so on, stories of people in unbelievably bad situations and how they made it out.

Another great book for survivors of trauma is *Waking the Tiger, Healing Trauma: The Innate Capacity to Transform Overwhelming Experiences,* by Peter A. Levine, which leads readers step by step to healing. And if you experienced childhood sexual abuse, *The Courage to Heal,* by Ellen Bass and Laura Davis, is a classic in the field.

There is light at the end of your tumult. —NAOMI JUDD

Two Wrongs Aren't Right

It's bad enough if somebody hurt you while you were growing up. But if you are continuing to let it mess with you now as an adult, *you* are allowing the abuse to happen all over again. How stupid is that? No matter how seriously you have been wronged, it's critical to your future well-being that you begin to deal with your anger and resentment once and for all.

Your parents raised you based on how they were raised. They probably did the best they could with what they knew back then. Now, with awareness, you can do much better.

I am a perfect example. Because I had witnessed my mom and dad's acrimonious divorce, I regrettably did some of the same things to Wy and Ashley when I divorced their dad. I hadn't yet forgiven their dad (or acknowledged my own responsibility in the relationship), so my blabbermouth behavior had a deleterious impact on the girls. I didn't realize that every child desperately needs to feel that each parent is good. After all, they gave you their genes. We have only one dad, one mom.

But Wynonna chose to break this negative cycle. Her pain from my parents' and my disastrous handling of our divorces caused her to consciously choose not to pass on our mistakes. She took the high road by not letting her divorce interfere with Elijah and Grace's perceptions of their dad. To reverse the curse, Wy practiced forgiveness and was changed. Now she is a changer and my grandkids are the changees.

*If there is righteousness in the heart, there will be beauty in
the character. If there is beauty in the character, there will be
harmony in the home. If there is harmony in the home, there
will be order in the nation. If there is order in the nation,
there will be peace in the world.* —CONFUCIAN PROVERB

Your Turn Now

To begin to reverse the curse in your life, answer the following
questions:

- What are the fleas on your own family members that bug
  you? What are the things you wish you could change about
  them? How can you change your own reactions? Do you
  see that others must see to the changing for themselves?

- OK now, what are the elephants on your shoulder—
  the issues you need to resolve? (I'll never lose this weight.
  Dad said I would never amount to anything. I lose my
  temper a lot.)

- Were you traumatized? Do you have troubling habits today
  that are a result of that experience? Do you have bad
  memories that haunt you? Would you say you have
  nightmares or flashbacks?

- What significant early events happened that shape and form
  your current beliefs about sexuality (for instance, were you
  caught masturbating)? How did your parents communicate
  to you about sex? What did your friends tell you?

- Imagine that you as a young child are standing in front of
  you right now. What did the younger you need that he or
  she didn't get?

- What self-defense mechanisms are you resorting to for emotional aspirin?

- What are the questions you need to ask to reverse the curse? Do you need help from someone specialized in dealing with the issues you face?

As you complete these mental and emotional exercises, it's time for a physical practice.

Begin by taking a deep belly breath, inhaling slowly, your belly expanding as you count to ten. (Most people take shallow breaths, and their belly doesn't rise.) Visualize that you are inhaling hope and new possibilities for the rest of your life. Feel where you're holding tension. Hold that thought/breath.

Now noisily exhale through your mouth. As you let go of your breath, release tightness and stress. Exhale what's old, tired, and not serving you.

Continue breathing this way as you go from the top of your head to the tip of your toes, consciously relaxing each part of your body. Did you know that through deep breathing you not only release mental and emotional stress, but eliminate 70 percent of your body toxins?

By the way, as I write this book I'm going to new places as well. By explaining these life-altering breakthroughs to you, I am reinforcing the knowledge that I've gathered over the past ten years. While sharing my discoveries about psychology, wellness, healing, success, and inner peace, I can't help but gain even further insights. We're getting better together, so let's keep breathing in what's possible and exhaling what's not working.

The process of letting go of what is completed or outgrown is absolutely essential in affirming life. One cannot engage with life if one is caught by the past sadness. It is the lack of connection with ongoing life that is harmful.—RACHEL NAOMI REMEN

5 You Can Be Anything You Want, but First You Have to Understand What's Standing in Your Way

A bad experience can result in a series of fallouts so that eventually you must find a different way to think. That's the awareness that Choice #5 brings—YOU CAN BE ANYTHING YOU WANT, BUT FIRST YOU HAVE TO UNDERSTAND WHAT'S STANDING IN YOUR WAY. This was a costly lesson for me to learn. I'll share a personal story so you can come up with your own example.

When I was a child, the people around me weren't much for expressing their feelings, so I began filling up a reservoir of emotions. Because Mom and Dad were such hardworking, blue-collar, everyday folks, they had literally no time or energy for artistic expression. I overcompensated by becoming a little drama queen.

On Christmas morning, for instance, I longed for a full-blown production. I'd plead with Daddy to stand at the bottom of the steps with our Bell & Howell movie camera, put "White Christmas" on the hi-fi, and film us like Cecil B. De Mille as we proceeded down the stairs as a happy family. I'd spend my allowance at the Saturday matinee, indulging my need for fantasy. Enraptured by theatrics, I pretended Daddy was Robert Mitchum and Mom the glamorous and passionate Susan Hayward.

When Brian died, we all retreated further into ourselves. In contrast, my emotionality took a quantum leap. Overflowing with my own feelings, I began channeling others' emotions. Raised in a sheltered environment, I was extremely naive, which turned into idealism. I developed unrealistic expectations of people, seeing only the good in everyone. (How about you? Are you an idealist or a cynic?)

While we should look for the good in everyone, I had blinders on to others' faults. An overactive fantasy life can get in the way of having our bearings in reality. In high school, I was so demure and submissive that I allowed that older boy to have his way with me and got pregnant. Later on, I failed to recognize obvious psychotic traits in the ex-con who beat me. I was not aware that my thinking was being clouded by idealism and fantasy, because the pattern was operating below the level of my conscious awareness.

This pattern of emotional behavior to the exclusion of rational thought continued until a rude wake-up call in my forties. I was betrayed financially. It took mounting evidence from financial advisers, who showed me black-and-white figures, before the underlying issue finally came to the surface. This costly financial and emotional mistake forced me to finally see what was standing in my way. I'd been idealizing this person to the exclusion of his many faults. The high price I paid forced me to recognize the subconscious pattern of being led blindly by idealism that had haunted me my whole life. As a consequence, I've become more realistic by judging others based on their behavior instead of my wishful fantasy. I'm choosing to see people for who they truly are. One important benefit is that my bank account is safer!

What about you? What are some present results of your ability to make choices by seeing others objectively?

Toto, I don't believe we're in Kansas anymore.
—DOROTHY, IN *THE WIZARD OF OZ*

Follow Your Yellow Brick Road

Wy, Ash, Larry, and I love to discuss the psychological overtones of movies and books. For example, the movie classic *The Wizard of Oz* has obvious symbolism. As Dorothy sings "Over the Rainbow," she yearns for a new, enchanted, mysterious place filled with opportunity. As the film opens, we see Dorothy's farm in flat Kansas, portrayed in boring black-and-white—a blatant symbol of stale dissatisfaction with her life. Dramatically, a tornado (crisis) transports her to the Technicolor Land of Oz, an imaginary place representing her subconscious mind filled with vivid adventures.

Sometimes it takes a catastrophic crisis like my financial betrayal (which resulted in a huge loss), an illness, or the loss of a relationship or job to force us to tap into our subconscious. Only then do we see old patterns for what they are and eventually awaken to our potential. Dorothy was counting on something outside herself to make her happy. Yet what she had to do was look within. The journey following the yellow brick road stands for the inner journey to self-discovery and self-actualization. Along the way Dorothy had to confront and destroy her demons, represented by the Wicked Witch. The Lion, the Tin Man, and the Scarecrow symbolize innate attributes of courage, caring, and brains. When she finally reaches the Emerald City (conscious awareness), Toto pulls back the curtain to expose an ordinary man posing as the Wizard.

Like Dorothy, you and I really are the magnificent and powerful wizards in our own lives. All the answers, adventures, and magic are waiting to be discovered in our very own subconscious minds. There truly is "no place like home." The seat of our soul is home.

Like Glinda the Good Witch, I'm here to remind you to click your heels because "you have the power all along." It's just a matter of looking within and discovering what is standing in your way. Sometimes we need to get out of our own way. It all begins and ends within ourselves.

He who looks outside dreams. He who looks inside wakes.
—CARL JUNG

Oh No, Not Again

Looking at what's standing in our way is crucial because, without our even being aware of it, emotional catalysts, past pain, and buried trauma can be programming how we're feeling, whatever we're believing, and how we're reacting in our present circumstances. Investigators from a diversity of fields have come up with strong evidence that shows that emotional stressors in early childhood set us up for later susceptibility to real organic disease. Your past can, without your knowledge, be directing you to make poor choices in relationships (marry the wrong person over and over again), finances (spend too much money on the wrong things), career (sabotage your jobs or underachieve), and other areas.

As I mentioned in previous chapters, someone with abuse in their childhood is likely to repeat abusive relationships later on. For instance, a girl who's the victim of incest may wind up subconsciously choosing an abusive lover or pimp. Having felt betrayed early on, she may feel like a worthless object. These feelings cause her to see all male-female relationships in terms of dominance and power. Anyone, male or female, in this situation will either want total control or be really submissive. Once emotions have been clouded by bad experiences, it's difficult for abused people to be in touch with, evaluate, and express their needs. Or they may be superaware of and attentive to their partner's needs and wants, but blind to that person's motivation. Until an abused individual gets to a higher level of awareness, any chance for a healthy relationship will be impossible.

Even if you have not been abused, it is essential to figure out what emotionally charged issues from childhood may be standing in your way. Otherwise, you're likely to continue whatever unhealthy, repetitive behavioral patterns were forced upon you when young.

Mr. Pain, it's you again.
You always seem to show up
When I'm all alone. That's when you move right in
And make yourself at home.
—"MR. PAIN," NAOMI JUDD

Emotion, Not Intellect, Drives All Behavior (Until We Become Conscious)

The reason you and I tend to repeat our past is that it's our emotions, not intellect, that drive so much of what we do. It's a result of our brain structure. Daniel Goleman says in his book on the subject, *Emotional Intelligence,* "We have two minds, one that thinks and one that feels." The emotional part of our brain is called the amygdala. The intellectual part of our brain is the neocortex. When anything happens, we receive the information first in our amygdala and have an emotional reaction before our intellect, the neocortex, even gets a chance to respond.

Our amygdala is the primitive, reptilian part of our brain. It is purely instinctual and irrational. It's genetically programmed to protect us from dangers. The problem is, though, that it can't differentiate very well. Early in our childhood, our amygdala decided what those dangers were and how best we should emotionally respond to them. Now, when you encounter something even remotely similar, that primal emotional programming in your amygdala goes off automatically. For instance, if your mother seemed threatening to you as a child, you might find as an adult that you respond defensively to all women. That's your amygdala trying to protect you. It sees "woman," and the program "Be afraid" instinctively turns on.

Many of our emotional reactions are like this. They come from biological patterns created back when we were very young. So this explains why even family members may have different emotional reactions to the same event. The original event that set our emotional programming was perceived very differently by each one.

That's why you and I can't control our emotionality—it happens automatically. However, the good news is that by understanding how our emotions originated, we can begin to regulate them. That's where our neocortex comes in. Once you and I identify a pattern behind a particular emotional reaction, we can stop and think. This engages our neocortex. For instance: "Is this woman in front of me dangerous like my mother, or am I just being triggered by my childhood?" When we become informed enough to use our neocortex, which rationally judges our emotional reaction, we can see the event for what it really is. Our response becomes appropriate and healthy.

Because of the way your mind is structured, if you are not aware of how you're vulnerable to being emotionally triggered, you'll never be able to make good choices. Your life will continue to be blindly driven by these primitive emotions. That's why choosing to stop and evaluate your emotions can improve your entire life. It greatly enhances your capacity to make wise choices for the sake of your future.

The number-one cause of mental illness is not knowing yourself.
—ANONYMOUS

How Are You Feeling?

Larry can testify that whenever Wy, Ash, and I are together, we're a "mob of emotions." I realize now it's because we feel safe enough to let our feelings be exposed in front of one another. As a result, we can be quite startling in our spontaneity and uninhibitedness.

Like us Judd gals, you are feeling some emotion in every moment. The four major ones are *fear, anger, sadness,* and *happiness.* Take a second now to ask yourself these important questions: Is your job fulfilling? Do you get the recognition you deserve? (If your answer is no, you are probably bored, listless, and resentful.) Are you in a relationship that's mutually sincere? (If not, you are unhappy, tired, anxious, and probably jealous.) Do your friends comfort and nourish you? (If not, they are draining and depleting you.) On a scale of one to ten, how spontaneous and uninhibited are you? Why?

My intention in this book is to get you to be 100 percent aware of your emotions. That means knowing precisely what you are feeling moment to moment and then choosing how to appropriately respond to those feelings. Once you're fully aware of how you feel, you get to choose appropriate ways to express it.

When you're genuinely tuned in to your feelings, you have heart knowledge. Heart knowledge is living out how you feel. Please allow yourself to really experience all your feelings! In doing so, your heart will guide you on your path, and your world will feel right. Blaze your own new path, and then leave a trail!

Look at every path closely and deliberately. Try it as many times as you feel necessary, and ask yourself, and yourself alone, one question: Does this path have a heart? If it does, it is good. If it doesn't, it is of no use. —CARLOS CASTANEDA

Becoming Aware of Your Feelings

You can learn to identify and begin to deal with your feelings in a healthy way. Psychologists refer to observing feelings and trying to figure out ways to deal with them as "emotional ruminating." Therapist Marsha Linehan describes a four-step process for ruminating. I have found it particularly useful and suggest highly that you consider it: observe, experience, remember, and love.

1 *Observe* Your Emotion

   ▪ NOTE its presence.

   ▪ Step BACK.

   ▪ Get UNSTUCK from the emotion.

2 *Experience* Your Emotion

   ▪ Feel it as a WAVE, coming and going.

   ▪ Try not to BLOCK, SUPPRESS, PUSH AWAY, or GET RID OF it.

   ▪ Don't try to KEEP it around, HOLD ON to it, or AMPLIFY it (make it worse than it is).

3   *Remember*: You Are Not Your Emotion

- Do not necessarily ACT on emotion.

- Remember times when you have felt DIFFERENT.

4   Practice *Loving* Your Emotion

- Don't JUDGE it.

- Practice WILLINGNESS to feel it.

- ACCEPT your emotion.

When you and I practice the four steps, we neither deny our feelings nor get endlessly caught up in them. This is good! We simply experience them, and learn what they have to teach us. This way we can move on. When we do this, we stay current and real with ourselves. We're much less likely to get caught in unconscious traps from our past.

Cherish your own emotions and never undervalue them.
—ROBERT HENRI

The Tip of the Iceberg

How we were raised is so important in determining whether we are now comfortable with our feelings and the emotional reactions we tend to have. We are products of both heredity (nature) and environment (nurture).

Looking at ourselves in a mirror is analogous to looking at an iceberg. We see only the tip. That's the product of our heredity, which determines our physical appearance. The majority of the iceberg is hidden under the fathoms of the sea. So it is with us as well. Our bone structure, hair, eye and skin color, shape of the face, and features come from our mother's and father's lineages of DNA. Dr. James Watson won the Nobel Prize in Physiology of Medicine for his famous codiscovery, with Francis Crick, of the double helix of DNA. Jim personally explained DNA to me as "the starter kit that builds our bodies." Both parents contribute their ancestors' genetic information to these building blocks—the tip of the iceberg.

For instance, DNA (nature) caused me to be born with porcelain white skin and petite, feminine features. Growing up, my nickname was China Doll. But because of my early environment (nurture), the deeper truth is that on the inside I'm very strong and unbreakable. The physical reflection I see in my own mirror doesn't reveal that I have a strong will and a heck of a lot of perseverance. You too are a combination of inner and outer.

If someone in our family had depression or anxiety, we may also be genetically vulnerable (nature). We may also be susceptible to depression if we were raised in a depressing or anxiety-provoking environment (nurture). Heredity loads and then hands you the gun; environment can pull the trigger.

Having a genetic link or maybe an unhealthy home environment increases our need to be aware of how our emotions drive bad habits. Early programming by heredity or the primitive brain can make us more likely to have separation anxiety disorder, post-traumatic stress disorder, social phobias, and the like. But if we become aware of the risks from heredity or bad early home events, then we can understand whatever's been standing in our way. This makes the difference. We can now choose to modify our behavior. This awareness becomes the source of our power to change the course of our future. We are self-determined instead of being driven by nature or our past. Then we have fewer of those "bad heir days."

*Experience is not what happens to a person. It is what
a person does with what happens to them.* —ALDOUS HUXLEY

Danger: Emotional Triggers Ahead

Pick one negative habit or harmful thing you do. That's real easy, right? OK, now identify the emotion triggering your behavior. Whoops! Much harder! For instance, if you are a nervous eater, next time you find yourself standing in front of an open refrigerator, push the pause button. Stop and take a deep breath. Just be there for as long as it takes and observe the circumstances. Are you physically hungry? Or did you just get an irritating phone call from your mother? Big difference. By recognizing the emotion behind your little everyday moments, you'll soon get the knack of spotting the emotional triggers creating your undesired behaviors. In this situation, the emotion of an upsetting phone call sent you running to the fridge for comfort. Eureka!

Also, in this case, are you aware that food contains mood-enhancing substances like tryptophan and caffeine? It's also a fact that foods have soothing emotional ties because mealtimes can evoke fond memories—not to mention that filling up with food supplies an actual tactile feeling of satisfaction. Unregulated emotional reactions can cause you to blindly carry out some pretty bad habits that can result in unhealthy things like obesity (unless you learn the causes and effects I'm explaining right now).

Are you *hungry, angry, lonely, tired?* HALT . . . because these four feelings can make you want food, cigarettes, drugs, or alcohol. (The HALT concept is used in various twelve-step programs.) Scientific evidence proves that identifying past unpleasant events that are triggering present behavior rewards you with the option to learn more skillful ways of reacting. Ultimately, you'll begin reacting quite differently. (P.S. Your mom isn't really there.)

It also helps to list the nice rewards you'll earn as you put these harmful triggers in their place. Think about your improved physical health, increased self-esteem, self-respect, and freedom from psychological distress and the associated guilt. These are huge rewards! Trust me, they're more emotionally gratifying than the Grammys. Get excited about them. Look forward to better psychosocial opportunities!

People I know personally who've lost weight, gone through rehab, or ditched a bad relationship say their breakthroughs happened after they finally realized that their behavior was all rooted in an attempt to feed some emotional or spiritual emptiness. When they became aware enough to fill the void with healthy pleasures, they had an amazing transformation. Do you have some void that needs filling? The twelve-step program for AA relies on surrendering to a higher power.

---

*When getting healthy became my goal, I discovered
that feeling 100 percent better physically, emotionally,
and mentally felt better than food tasted.*

—DEBBIE AIKENS, LONGTIME JUDD FAN WHO LOST EIGHTY POUNDS

Is It Possible You Are a Wound Addict?

One of the most interesting people I came across during my foray into the ways people heal was an expert on why some folks can't seem to discover what's standing in their way. Therefore they don't heal or move on. Caroline Myss, a former journalist and theologian, is a respected pioneer in the intriguing field of energy medicine. Caroline spent time explaining to me how some people actually identify with their physical illness or emotional suffering. They become stuck as "wound addicts." Interesting stuff!

Did you ever consider how you may be using your disease or emotional wound as an excuse—an excuse to avoid honest communication, feel important, or cover up some failure—or as an alibi to get out of meeting the expectations of a mate, a job, or your own potential? Rather than doing the work of discovering what's standing in your way, could you be getting even more attached to being broken or sick?

Wound addicts use their problems or illnesses to manipulate others and get attention. They wallow around and marinate in them. The longer they stay identified with their wound, the longer it persists.

My favorite example of Caroline Myss's philosophy comes from another sagacious healer, Dr. Gladys McGarey. Gladys was the first president of the American Holistic Medical Association. In a lecture I attended, Gladys detailed her frustration about a patient suffering from lupus. The patient hadn't figured out what was standing in her way, so she'd not been able to make significant progress. At the close of one of their sessions, they walked out into the parking lot, where Gladys spied the patient's license plate. It proclaimed, LUPUS. This woman had become identified with her disease! She qualifies as a wound addict. No wonder she could not get better.

When Gladys noticed my smiling reaction in the front row as she told this story, she asked for comments. I reported that while I was ill I'd gone to renew Larry's and my car registrations.

I spontaneously chose personalized plates for our cars. The words FAITH and HOPE immediately came to my mind since aiming for a positive outcome is the way my mind works. It's always in the forefront of my thinking. As Samuel Johnson said, "Hope is itself a species of happiness, and perhaps the chief happiness which this world affords."

If you or someone you know qualifies as a wound addict, I can recommend all of Caroline Myss's books, particularly *Anatomy of the Spirit* and *Why People Don't Heal and How They Can.* Only by understanding what's standing in our way can we enable true healing and happiness to take place. We deserve to move beyond past wounds.

To change your life, start immediately. Do it flamboyantly, no exceptions. —WILLIAM JAMES

Your Turn Now

Try this Mirror of Truth exercise in privacy. It may seem uncomfortable (and even downright bizarre) at first, but it's been proven to be a powerful psychological method for self-discovery.

> *Start your day by looking into a mirror and asking yourself, "Mirror, mirror on the wall, who am I, after all?" Repeat this out loud when you're in the bathroom or anywhere private. Take a few minutes to thoughtfully delve below the surface for real "self-reflection." Begin with labels like these:*

Who am I?

I am _____ *'s offspring.*

I am _____ *'s sibling.*

I am ———————— *'s spouse.*

I am ———————— *'s parent.*

I am ———————— *'s employee/boss.*

I am ———————— *(what else?).*

Now penetrate the surface:

1   *In which role have I been miscast? (Example: I don't really want to have to work. I'd rather be a stay-at-home mom. Or: I'm unhappy in my marriage. My needs have evolved.)*

2   *What do I not like about myself? (Examples: I wish I had more education. I'm afraid people will find out I'm not smart enough. I can't control my eating. I weigh too much and would like to be thinner.)*

3   *What do I like about myself? (Say something descriptive like "I take really good care of my family," "I have a great sense of humor," "I see the good in others," "I'm optimistic.")*

4   *How well acquainted am I with my emotional life? Am I at the mercy of my feelings all the time? Do I have a hard time knowing how I feel? Do I find myself angry out of the blue? Or sad? Am I depressed?*

5   *Do I cover over my feelings with drugs, alcohol, cigarettes, overwork, eating, shopping, trying to please others?*

6   What's missing from my life that I'd like to add?
    (A better social life? Someone to love? Solitude?
    More downtime?)

7   Who or what is stopping me from doing this?
    (Habits? Negative feelings? Pressure from others?)

8   If you were introduced to God, how would you describe
    yourself? What would you be trying to hide? Do you love
    that part of you you're trying to hide anyway? Do you
    resent having to fulfill an expectation?

9   Tell the mirror you love yourself.

10 What emotion are you feeling at the end of this exercise?
    Are you willing to look at and allow any feelings that may
    come up from now on? Would you like to have a solid,
    no-holds-barred relationship with yourself?

Every time you study your features in a mirror (probably
looking for faults), keep excavating your feelings. This is
important, so ask questions about whether you feel safe in
your most important relationships. Who do you trust the
most? What's a frustrating part of your daily life? Look
back on your day and think about feelings that sprang up.
As you dig up and come face-to-face with these feelings,
potent emotional reactions will start to tumble out.
Anytime you start to feel uncomfortable, you'll know you've
hit a nerve. So stop. Stay with that emotion for a minute.
Let it wash over you. It offers valuable information. Ask,
"What's going on?" out loud to the mirror. Getting straight
with yourself is a crucial step to self-discovery.

I'm not denying that this exercise may be uncomfortable. But to be all you can, you have to know what's standing in your way. I had to do some of these exercises before I began to write this book. Don't feel bad, Moses was a basket case once. So was I.

I knew Jose Menendez, who was killed with his wife, Kitty, by their sons, Lyle and Eric. Jose struck me as a conceited egomaniac. He reeked of Cuban cigars and tyrannical arrogance. When I watched the murder trial, I was struck by how Lyle and Eric had massacred their own parents out of greed. The two young men had not realized that it wasn't their parents who were standing in their way, it was their inability to grow and change. Today they are rotting in prison.

You and I are still free, thank God. But if we don't deal with what's blocking our chance for happiness, we create an emotional prison.

Did families really bow their heads to pray?
Did Daddy never really go away?
Grandpa, tell me 'bout the good ol' days. . . .

—"GRANDPA," JUDDS SONG

6 Become a Detective and Investigate Your Past

*I*t was during my parents' painful divorce that I discovered the transformative power of Choice #6: BECOME A DETECTIVE AND INVESTIGATE YOUR PAST. I love the word "transformation." "Trans" means "above," "across." "Form" refers to your limits, shapes, boundaries. The suffix "ion" means "the experience of." When we experience a transformation, a changing of the shape we're in, we can have the experience of rising above our previous limits. That's what happened to me.

Still living in Hollywood, I'd flown home to Kentucky to see what in the world was going on with my parents. Daddy picked me up at the airport and we stopped for a bite to eat. It felt unusual to be alone with him.

In the privacy of the restaurant booth, he slowly related his side of the split. It was the first time that Daddy talked about his feelings. It was also the first time I ever considered him as a man as well as my father. As he spoke, there was this beat where we were on the same level, as adults. As preposterous as it may sound now, in that moment it became clear that he was going through many of the same issues that I was facing. He was in midlife and I was in my late twenties, but we were asking the same soul-searching questions: How did I get into this fix? Where do I go next in my life? (Have you ever considered that your parents are individuals with their own issues to deal with?)

Same thing with Mom. Along with searching for clues as to what had killed her marriage, she was trying to put her life back together. How would she make a living for herself? Would she ever find the right man? She too echoed the exact issues I was struggling with. Over a pot of coffee at the kitchen table, I found myself thrust into the role of her friend. It wasn't me running in the kitchen to grab a soda from the refrigerator while she sat chatting confidentially about adult things with Aunt Roberta or Kitty Southers. I was the one in the chair where Roberta and Kitty usually sat. Having never supported herself, she was scared. Mom seemed convinced she had no job skills. Then, by looking into her past, we realized that cooking was one of her passions and talents. Mom got a job as a cook on a riverboat. She also eventually married the riverboat captain!

As a star witness to Mom and Dad's messy divorce, I had many of my long-held beliefs obliterated. They didn't have all the answers after all. In fact, my own parents seemed as lost as I was! My assumption that they would be together forever was also thrown out. There were all sorts of disturbing concerns about money, loyalty, what would become of our beloved house that I had grown up in, where we would spend our holidays, and so on. Every divorce is the death of a miniature civilization.

Although it was painful, in an emotional sense, I came to life during their divorce. It took my parents splitting apart for me to accept fully my separateness from them. Since I was now divorced too, I had my maiden name, Judd, reinstated. And in a symbolic acknowledgment that I was now my own person, I changed my first name from Diana to Naomi. I also began to think of my mother by her first name, Polly. The mental exercise allowed me to see her situation more objectively, through the eyes of a caring friend, and was helpful in understanding her needs. (Try this yourself: consider your folks by their first names and view them through the eyes of a contemporary. How does that change your perceptions of them?)

I bailed before the actual court divorce proceeding. I wouldn't be put in the middle by testifying for one or the other. I returned to California, deciding instead to become my own judge and jury as I investigated my own case. Up until that point in my life, as you know, my own choices hadn't been serving me too well. I began to uncover clues to the similarities between my parents' challenges and my own.

It's not what happens to us that matters as much as what we do with it. Despite the pain I felt over my parents' divorce, I used what I was learning to positive effect. I dissected my parents' individual strengths and weaknesses. As a result, I began to see how my personality had been influenced by them. Doing this detective work was the only way to get a grip on how early influences were still playing out in my daily choices. Once I became aware, I could make different choices.

Nothing fortuitous happens in a child's world. There are no accidents. Everything is connected with everything else and everything can be explained by everything else. . . . For a young child, everything that happens is a necessity. —JOHN BERGER

Don't Let Nature Run Its Curse

When I became a detective in my past, here's what I uncovered. Daddy—Glen Judd—was your basic hardworking, country kind of guy. He ran his own gas station, smoked Camels, drove a pickup truck, read Mickey Spillane novels, and watched boxing on Friday nights. I still remember his manly scent of grease and Lava soap. I could recognize the sound of Daddy's black pickup no matter where I was playing in our neighborhood. When he'd come home in the evening from working at Judd's Friendly Ashland Service Station, I would stop whatever I was doing, rush to our front gate, grab him around the waist, and tell him how much I loved him.

But Daddy was the product of his own upbringing. He was from a time when any demonstration or expression of emotion from a man was considered unnatural and even effeminate. Guys like my daddy were strong and silent in those days. He loved me very much, but he never knew how to return my ebullient emotions. Our ancestors were reticent farmers with old-fashioned beliefs about roles for males and females. Daddy worked like an absolute brute over at that gas station so that I could have a good, safe home, plenty of food, piano lessons, and even braces on my teeth. That was typical, in those days, of how men showed love for their family.

When my girlfriend Reba McEntire showed me around her home one night after supper, she proudly pointed out a picture of her dad, Clark. I knew that he'd come out of the rodeo circuit in their small town in Oklahoma. Reba smiled as she began to explain how art imitates life. Her number-one country single at the time was "The Greatest Man I Never Knew." She related how her father had also been one of those typically hardworking, unaffectionate, distant fathers. But he'd recently undergone surgery and, on the way into the operating room, had surprised her by saying, "I love you."

Growing up, Reba and I both craved more affection and expression, so we've compensated as adults by becoming professional communicators. Since I was constantly trying to get my daddy's attention and win his affections, I evolved into a creative and expressive child. I became an extrovert.

Now that I've became a detective in my life, I realize that this experience as a child is what led me to becoming a performer. I remember feeling like a big piñata walking around hoping someone would break me open so I could spill out my emotions and secrets. The first prophetic entry my mom made into my baby book was "She has a vivid imagination." Daddy's strong work ethic also made an indelible impression on me. His meticulously clean station offered great, friendly service and was always chosen Ashland Oil Station of the Year. Everything I witnessed about how Daddy took pride in his job I still emulate in my own work habits to this very day. He'd say, "Be the labor great or small, do it well or not at all." My daddy died of kidney failure in 1984.

As adults, we sometimes wind up compensating for what we were lacking as children, just as I compensated by being demonstrative when my daddy wasn't. That was true for my mother. Pretty Polly, my good-humored, redheaded mama, was devoted to raising our family. It consisted of my brothers, Brian and Mark, and my sister, Margaret. I was the eldest, and all of us were two years apart. My whole childhood was consistently secure. I felt safe, cared for, and valuable. Besides being an extrovert, you may have noticed that I am determined and self-sufficient, with a strong sense of purpose about the importance of serving others.

Mom had a very difficult, fractured childhood. At an early age she saw that she couldn't depend on her folks, so she learned to fend for herself. Therefore, Mom had a strong need to compensate for what she'd missed. She broke the cycle by creating the family and home she'd wanted. She also instilled in all us kids a sense of responsibility and civic duty. Until recently Mom was a city commissioner serving her fellow citizens of Ashland.

I remember her standing over me when I was a little girl, teaching, "Daughter of mine, you can do anything if you just set your mind to it" and "Judd women always land on their own two feet." Mama also instructed me never to let anybody tell me who I am. She always encouraged us four kids to live our own lives— "To thine own self be true." Mom's a survivor of heartbreak and tragedy. Her life personifies her philosophy of family, self-reliance, and service. Today, she's happy and well respected, and still lives in the house I was raised in.

My Judd grandparents, aunts, and uncles lived on a remote farm in rural Louisa, Kentucky. I see how growing up around them in Appalachia has given me an abiding love for the outdoors, the natural world, and animals. Today Wy, Elijah, and Grace; Ash and her husband, Dario; and Larry and I share neighboring farms deep in a pristine valley of the Tennessee countryside. I chose this unspoiled setting and quiet lifestyle to re-create the blissful days spent as a child in the country with the Judd clan. Back then, my grandmommy Sally Ellen; my granddaddy Ogden Judd; and my dear aunts Pauline, Evelyn, Toddie, Faith, and Ramona would put me up on the kitchen table at their farmhouse, where I would dance and sing my heart out. They'd whistle, cheer, and stomp their feet. I see now how this really boosted my self-esteem.

Decades later, I would find myself performing in concert halls around the world, singing and dancing just as I had when I was a little girl. My family's love and encouragement helped me think of myself in that winner category by the time I was three.

As a result of writing a song about my great-grandparents Elijah and Fanny ("Guardian Angels"), we did a family genealogy. I gave the results to everyone for Christmas one year. (Genealogists live in the past lane.)

Do you know your family tree? Consider finding it out from living relatives and recording them talking about their memories of growing up. Ask them to share the meaning of their mementoes. Make copies of old photos. The greatest gift any family can give is roots and wings.

Children have never been good at listening to their elders, but they have never failed to imitate them. —JAMES BALDWIN

Chase Your Own Tale

Just as with me, the beliefs that you hold to today are the result of your own unique memories and experiences, which began developing from the moment you were born. You're as totally original as a snowflake or a fingerprint.

As young children, we were blank slates who mimicked whatever our parents did. We bought into everything they said, whether it was in our best interest or they were merely unconsciously reacting to what had been handed down to them. Much like a lump of clay being molded, our personality and character slowly took shape through these interactions over the first years of life. Every experience, from how we were treated or mistreated to how people related to us, created our personalities and beliefs today. Indeed, psychologists say that by the time we are eight, our personality and temperament are fully formed.

Those early individual conversations, interactions, and reactions within your home formed the microcosm of your existence. As the motto on American money says, *E pluribus unum*—"Out of many, one." The unique individual you are has been formed by many layers of influences, most predominantly those of your primary caretakers. The beliefs you formed out of that early microcosm determine how you are wired to perceive the macrocosm of the world now.

Based on those early experiences, for instance, we feel like either winners or losers; we're blessed with a healthy self-concept or cursed with low self-esteem. If you had good experiences with your parents as a child, you'll be more apt today to respond favorably to authority figures like teachers, firemen, policemen, and bosses. You may have even become one. On the other hand, if your parents physically abused or neglected you, your perception of authority is probably skewed. You may be rebellious and have trouble following rules. Which category do you fall into?

As adults, the more we become aware of what happened to us as children, the more we can choose to separate from that early imprinting, if that is appropriate. Finding out what took place in our formative years is the first step in discovering who we are now. For the more we understand what our unique childhood tracks were, the more we can consciously choose whether we want to be on that particular train anymore.

Children begin by loving their parents. After a time they judge them. Rarely, if ever, do they forgive them. —OSCAR WILDE

Looking Back Through Adult Eyes

You couldn't choose the family you were born into, but now you're older and wiser. You see the world with adult eyes. Just as you've outgrown the clothes you wore as a child, you've now evolved to a greater capacity for understanding. That's why you're interested in this book.

No matter what happened to us as children, as adults we must take responsibility for the choices we make. Psychologists say that after thirty, we can no longer blame our parents for our failures and shortcomings. Darn! It's so easy and fun! (Ash and Wy, take note.) That's because, although you can't change what happened to you as a child, you can revisit the past, view it through informed adult eyes, take the lessons, and make conscious new choices based on your evolved understanding.

Karen, a friend from a highly dysfunctional home, has a mom and dad who are very mean-spirited people. They were horrible parents, and she describes them as "cell mates in an institution called marriage." As an adult, Karen went to therapy to figure out why her mom and dad are screwed up, so she wouldn't repeat the pattern with her own kids. I so admire her! Karen decided to change her mind and thereby changed her world. She's turned out to be a well-adjusted adult and tolerates her parents (from a distance). By becoming a detective in her past, she freed herself to move forward.

Truth is circumstantial. —RAM DASS

Your Turn Now

Were you thinking your past was a closed case? Well, you'd better reopen the file and review it carefully! Let's solve the riddle of who you are now so you can become who you want to be next. We want your autobiography to have a happy ending. *So, come out, come out, whoever you are!*

Think back. See if you can figure out who and what influenced who you are and what you believe about yourself.

- Who were the most powerful influences around you during that time?

- Did your parents nurture and encourage you? Hug and kiss you? If you spilled your milk at the table as a child, were you scolded, or did your parents just smile and say, "Whoopsy Daisy"?

- When you tried to speak, were you listened to and were your needs acknowledged? Were you slighted, or ignored? Was there face-to-face contact? Were you encouraged to try new things?

- How were you punished?

- Who inspired you by believing in you?

- What was the emotional climate in your home growing up—peaceful, happy, bitter, angry?

- Did your parents instruct you in manners? Can you recall a typical mealtime and what foods were served?

- What special gifts do you remember being given?

- What big news happened within your family that stands out?

- What personality traits did you get from your dad? From your mom?

- Do you classify yourself as an extrovert or an introvert? To what can you attribute this in your childhood?

- You can learn a lot about your childhood by looking back at your baby pictures, home movies, or baby book. Were you in clean clothes? Were you smiling? Were there toys? Was the background orderly?

- Was your neighborhood a safe place? Did you know your neighbors?

- Describe what your mom and dad would do in a typical day. What's your favorite memory of each of them? How did your father express his emotions?

- What signals did they send out about their marriage? If your parents were arguing, did one of them try to recruit you to their side? Or were you put in the middle as a mediator of disagreements? Did they argue behind closed doors? Did they openly show affection?

- What do you know about your parents' childhoods? How about your grandparents'? How did you feel about your family as a whole? (We're going to look at siblings in the next chapter.) When you are assessing these early memories, also think about your extended family, including grandparents, aunts, uncles, and cousins.

- What was the best part of your childhood? The worst?

- Did you have a pet? What was its name?

- Who were your playmates, and what did you do together? What do you remember about their families? Do you stay in contact with any of them?

- Picture your early home in your mind. What do you remember of its rooms and furnishings?

- Looking back, name two ways your family shaped your beliefs and values. For instance, my daddy passed on his ethic of hard work; Mom, her belief in the importance of family.

- What was important in your home? Did your family have rituals—praying together, eating together?

- How is your own family now different from your family of origin?

- Do you feel accountable for your behavior? Why or why not?

It's fascinating to discover how you've developed your likes and dislikes, even what kind of environment you're drawn to live in. You may not recognize it, but every day your childhood is still influencing your life! The more we understand our past, the more we can go on to make conscious choices that can create healthier emotions and more pleasurable and satisfying daily lives.

All parents want their children to have a better life than they did. It's a tribute to our parents that we not only carry on their good traits but learn from their shortcomings. We do it not only for ourselves, but for those who will come after us. Don't let your heir down!

Life is a voyage that is homeward bound. —HERMAN MELVILLE

7 Personality: It's All Relative

*C*an you guess, besides parental influence, how your person-ality was formed? Birth order! An experience as adult roommates with my sister led to this awareness—Choice #7: PERSONALITY: IT'S ALL RELATIVE. Just like the beat of recognition at the restaurant when I came to see my dad as a man as well as my father, or that all-night kitchen tête-à-tête when Mom and I shared divorce woes woman-to-woman, there came a moment when I viewed my sister, Margaret, through adult eyes.

Margaret, who's six years younger than I, had to live out her teens during the tumultuous time following Brian's death. She rebelled by marrying the captain of the basketball team and immediately got pregnant. In quick order Margaret was divorced and back living at home with her newborn. It wasn't a good situation, since Mom and Dad were on the verge of their divorce. So I invited her to come out to Hollywood and live with me. We celebrated her daughter, Erin's, first birthday together as single working moms.

Margaret and I were renting a house off Sunset Strip. One night when we were entertaining friends, the Moody Blues were playing on the stereo and the sangria was flowing freely when someone asked Margaret how she was making the transition from Appalachia to Hollywood. I was floored by her response.

The contrast in our sentiments allowed me to gain a whole new understanding of my "baby sister." To hear her tell it, Margaret had escaped the confines of a small-town mind-set. Southern California was a welcome paradise. I cherished my nostalgic recollections of our Norman Rockwell community, but Margaret never looked back. In that moment, it was clear that despite our having the same genetic makeup and being raised under the same roof, Margaret and I were distinctly different individuals. Later I understood that the differences between us had to do with our birth order, and armed with that understanding, I saw how important it is to stay current. Do you have ongoing adult relationships with your siblings? Or do you still have frozen mental snapshots of them as kids?

As the firstborn in my family, I was the Judd family banner carrier. Having no competition, I was talkative and bossy. Brother Brian, two years younger, was quite amiable and sociable. Mark was a textbook quiet, reactive third child. Mark got Brian's hand-me-down clothes. When school began, Mark's first identity with teachers was as Naomi and Brian's little brother. He was introspective and attached to Brian. As the youngest, Margaret benefited from more relaxed parents thanks to older siblings who'd broken in the parents and fought to establish ground rules.

By the time I had to move out to go live with my new husband's family, at age seventeen, my personality was formed. My beliefs about myself and how I related to others were set. Because I'd enjoyed a stable, loving childhood, I had trust in and respect for others. I took happy memories with me. At the same time, however, Margaret was only eleven, and her formative years were being marred by the chaos of my pregnancy and departure, the death of Brian, and our now feuding parents. She was caught in the cross fire. Even though Margaret and I are blood kin, we experienced radically different childhoods. Therefore we have different personalities. I conformed and she rebelled. By the time each of us left home, we took very different realities and temperaments with us. So did you and your siblings.

As I listened to Margaret describing her experiences growing up, I learned more about her and adjusted some opinions. That prompted self-reflection as well. I stepped back and began a more objective assessment of my own memories. As a result, Margaret and I pieced our memories together and have a more complete picture of our family life.

Recognizing the crucial influence the timing of birth order has in contributing to our memories, experiences, and personalities is an important part of learning from our past. Rather than assuming it has no effect, when we choose to look at the dynamics created by birth order, we gain greater understanding of how we tick, as well as our siblings. This can shed light on old subconscious patterns. And it grants us the freedom to get rid of these hang-ups.

I just found out my mom and dad are first cousins. No wonder I look so much like myself. —ROGER MILLER, SONGWRITER

The Ties That Bind

I became so curious about how birth order forms our personality that I met with an expert on the subject, Frank Sulloway, Ph.D., a psychologist at Stanford University. Frank explained that as toddlers, when we jockey for position within the family structure, we invent clever strategies to get our parents' attention and win their approval. This means that the order in which you were born into your family has a strong bearing on determining your personality traits as well as your socialization skills.

For the firstborn, says Dr. Sulloway, parental expectations are pretty high. The child is often expected to set an example and is usually given responsibilities. Therefore, firstborns start out in life by identifying with power and authority. They take the first available roles, like proving themselves with scholastic achievement and responsibility. They tend to be organized, assertive, socially dominant, ambitious, conscientious, and achievement oriented. Tough minded, they might also be defensive and jealous of their status. A high percentage of U.S. presidents (like George Washington) and world leaders (like Winston Churchill, Stalin, Mussolini, and Mao Zedong) were firstborns. Twenty-one of the first twenty-three astronauts were firstborns. Many people in entertainment, like Steven Spielberg, John Wayne, Bette Davis, and Katharine Hepburn, were born first in their families.

Siblings go out of their way to be different from one another, so second-born children start early on trying to contrast. They're going to be different because they want to be separate and autonomous. They question the status quo and are more likely to become explorers, inventors, iconoclasts, or heretics. They're rarely able to endure strict leadership from others. Madonna and Fidel Castro are famous second-borns. Second-borns are often more cooperative than the firstborns (another way to be different) and turn out to be peacemakers, like Dr. Martin Luther King, Jr. They are also sociable and adventuresome, like David Letterman. Boy, all these traits describe my second-born, Ashley!

By the time third children come along, they may feel squeezed out of a position of significance. They're really sandwiched if other children come along later. They're too small to confront the two older siblings, which causes them to develop more of a take-it-or-leave-it attitude. They tend to be flexible and even-tempered (like Tom Hanks) and might even wind up being fighters of injustice. The third child may come at a time when there is so much going on in the home that there is not a lot of time to spend individually on him or her. There may not be as much money either, since there are more mouths to feed and bodies to clothe.

The youngest child in the family obviously has the older siblings acting like mothers and fathers, continually trying to educate and take care of him or her. Youngest children become creative, humorous, and affectionate. They are often risk takers. As the baby, they hold a special position and never get dethroned, since they're the last child. They may gravitate toward careers in working with people. Youngest children may stay spoiled their whole life and may dream of huge plans that rarely work out—that is, unless they're comedians, like Jim Carrey, Rosie O'Donnell, Jay Leno, and Jerry Seinfeld!

An only child gets 100 percent attention from both parents, who may tend to be overprotective. Onlies are self-confident and usually do well in school. They tend to achieve high positions in life, like Oprah Winfrey. Parents often encourage them to choose a safe profession (like golf for Tiger Woods) over something such as a contact sport. Growing up, they likely prefer adult company and use adult language. In their adult life they'll continue wanting to be the center of attention, like only child Robin Williams.

Obviously, major events or time lapses in between children cause exceptions to these birth order generalizations. Unusual chronological sequencing (like long stretches between siblings) or crises (as when a child is born after one dies) create what's known as *psychological* birth order. This may result in children having "only" personalities even if they are in a big family, or survivor guilt that lingers a lifetime if unexamined.

> *We can never establish with certainty what part of our relationships with others is the result of our emotions—love, antipathy, charity or malice—and what part is predetermined by the constant power play among individuals.* —MILAN KUNDERA

Everybody Has His Own Reality

It's only natural to expect our blood relatives to think and act just like us. But they don't, and now you see it's not at all possible, due to birth order! This is a huge concept every family needs to grasp. If four people witness a car wreck, you'll get four different versions of what happened. The same thing is true for family life. Now every time Margaret and I share realities, we come closer to understanding the whole story of our family's dynamics. Then, all of a sudden, as Yogi Berra says, "The past isn't what it used to be."

Often, as adults, we have trouble viewing our siblings as contemporaries. After we move into our own homes and create our own families, we tend to lose touch. Therefore, we carry around frozen mental snapshots of our brothers and sisters—the bossy girl, the funny boy, the quiet one, the smart one—and this stands in the way of our seeing who they are now. The more we keep in touch with one another, however, the more chance we have to update those early impressions.

It's likely that you and your siblings will outlive your folks, so your sibling relationships are the longest you will have. Allowing one another to express and honor individual truths about what happened in your early home life may be tough going at first, but ultimately it can lead to your becoming lifelong friends if you aren't already.

Since we've become enlightened by all this research into sibling relationships, my sister, "Maggot"—I mean Margaret—and I try to take an annual sisterhood trip. Our first year we went to the desert in Tucson, Arizona, and it was such a blast! We discovered the pleasure of each other's company without our husbands and kids. One year we attended a four-day seminar on the psychology of healing in Hilton Head, South Carolina. It was richly fertile soil for us to continue to grow together as best friends. We've reconnected as contemporaries.

Brother Mark and I take a walk around the park where we played as children every time we go to visit Mom in Ashland, Kentucky. "Marky"—I mean Mark—and I stay tuned in to each other as adults. I'm smiling 'cause I got him for my brother and laughing 'cause there's nothing he can do about having me for his sister.

When my husband saw how beneficial my adult sibling outings were, he got his own two brothers together for a golfing weekend. To Larry's surprise, he discovered that Reggie and Donald had very different takes on childhood events. Something he'd all but forgotten was the single most impactful event in Reggie's upbringing. One person's trauma could be a blip on the radar screen for another. Now I notice Larry picking up the phone more often to check in with his brothers.

My idea of a happy family is close-knit, loving relatives who live in the next city! —GEORGE BURNS

Call a Truce in the Sibling War

When was the last time you spoke to your siblings? You and I will never be whole unless we clean up unresolved sibling issues from our past. Plus, we all need every bit of affection and support from those who understand us and share our past. So if you have drifted away from your siblings or been in out-and-out conflict, perhaps it's time to reestablish your relationship.

If you decide, as Larry and I did, that you do want to reconnect with your siblings as adults, I advise establishing up front that you're not getting together to beat one another up about old issues. Agree that nobody is allowed to play old tapes or try to settle old scores. It's not about being right. You're meeting in the here and now with a commitment to connection. Your hope and goal are to rebuild trust and express forgiveness, if needed.

Prepare for reconciliation by considering how your separate realities are keeping you from seeing eye to eye. Factor in how a dramatic change like divorce, death, illness, unemployment, a long-distance move, or a remarriage may have impacted each sibling. Consider their age at the time of the event. Be aware of differences in genetics, personality development, and temperament. Then plan to start meeting on neutral ground, doing an activity—going to a concert, attending a sporting event, shopping, or seeing a movie. Commit to enjoying the companionship with "relative" ease.

Then when you feel you're both ready to approach a potentially tricky topic, pick your time and place. Establish communication rules ahead of time. (Our family finally learned an excellent way to allow the other person to have their say. It acknowledges their feelings without denying yours. We say, "Tell me more about your perception, because that's not my reality.") Then silently listen without interruption. Treat your sibling as you would a friend. Expect him or her to grant you the same consideration.

By compiling everyone's perceptions of your family's past, you can put together all those missing pieces of a complex emotional jigsaw puzzle. It will allow you to see the whole picture, maybe for the first time.

The truth is not simply what you think. It is also the circumstance in which it was said, and to whom, why, and how it was said.
—VÁCLAV HAVEL, FORMER PRESIDENT OF THE CZECH REPUBLIC

Your Turn Now

Looking with new eyes at your relationships with your brothers and sisters in light of all these new clues to their personalities, what insights do you come up with? I'll bet your feelings toward your siblings change once you start understanding their distinctly unique realities.

Here are some questions to consider:

- Are you unconsciously chained to an inaccurate conclusion about some event in your childhood that made you feel slighted?

- Could you be falsely believing there is something lacking or superior in yourself, when it's purely a manifestation of birth order?

- Where siblings were concerned, did you feel that you got preferential treatment?

- Did you get along well or fight a lot?

- Were there nicknames?

- Did you, like me, have a sibling who died young? How did that impact you and the rest of the family?

- How do your relationships with your siblings carry over into the other relationships in your life?

I hope this knowledge inspires you. Once you see how important timing and early sibling interactions were in forging the blueprint of your personality, you can begin correcting and updating that blueprint. This can perhaps help us put our early hurts into perspective and heal. Or it can illuminate a destructive pattern we've been carrying with us into the present. And hopefully it can bring us closer to those who shared our childhood with us. A loving family is one of life's greatest rewards.

Forgiveness is not an occasional act;
it is a permanent attitude. —MARTIN LUTHER KING, JR.

8 Know Forgiveness, Know Peace— No Forgiveness, No Peace

I confess—forgiveness was one of my greatest challenges. I would have rather run naked through a Teamsters meeting. But there came a day when I couldn't run from it any longer. Here's what led up to my embracing Choice #8: KNOW FORGIVENESS, KNOW PEACE—NO FORGIVENESS, NO PEACE.

When I got pregnant unexpectedly at seventeen, my thinking was clouded by the family drama going on around me. My reasoning was typically immature. I felt personally responsible for the subsequent death of my brother from cancer and the divorce of my parents. If only I hadn't subjected everyone to my sinful mistake. If only I had been able to find the right doctor for Brian. If only I had still been at home to help Mom and Dad find a way to communicate. *Coulda, woulda, shoulda.* Bad words. I was drowning in guilt.

Back then I knew nothing about the practice of forgiveness. When I wound up stuck in dead-end jobs in Hollywood, patted on the butt and paid in pennies, I'd mentally beat myself up for not going to college. I'll never forget how demeaning it was standing in line for my welfare checks and food stamps. I didn't have a car, and each time I had to take my sick children to the pediatrician on the city bus, I felt even more incompetent as a provider. I felt like LOSER was stamped on my forehead. The more I beat myself up, the lower I sank into remorse.

Raising Wy and Ashley by myself while working to keep a jar of peanut butter on our table was exhausting. There was no one to give me a hug or a word of encouragement. I resented their fathers for leaving me in this fix. So not only was I beating myself up mentally, I was expending precious energy on frustration and bitterness toward them.

So one day in my early thirties, I realized it was all too much. The girls needed every drop of me. The old nagging guilt and current resentment were too costly. In order to create a better life for myself and my daughters, I had to economize on any negative emotions. I chose to cut out the self-flagellation and bitterness that had been depleting my spirit.

Ultimately, learning to forgive myself and others was one of the most liberating breakthroughs I had. I let go of the toxic emotions that were dragging me down. I knew peace.

He who conquers others is strong. He who conquers himself is victorious. —LAO-TZU

Forgiveness Isn't an Emotion, It's a Decision

News flash! Forgiveness is not for the person who offended you. It is for, and all about, *you*. In order for me to begin to forgive, I had to wrap my mind in this very important truth.

Second, forgiveness doesn't mean you have to deny what happened, and you certainly don't have to condone or forget the wrong. Rather, forgiveness is choosing to stop your vengeance from diminishing you by dragging you down to someone else's level. Have you ever considered how holding a grudge allows the other person's pathological behavior to make you stuck or sick?

There is evil in this world. It's not just a concept or theory. Evil is very real. That makes forgiveness very tricky. But by forgiving, we overcome evil with our goodwill.

Whenever I have trouble forgiving someone, I remember that the person who hurt me probably was wounded when young and still doesn't know the lifesaving choices I am discussing in this book. That's when I use this visualization: I imagine the persons who have wronged me as helpless, innocent infants. They're uncomfortable and crying, yet nobody brings them a bottle, diaper, or blanket. No one is bonding with them emotionally. This means they can't ever feel valued or worthy. Their first sense of their world is of a scary and unsafe place. They don't trust themselves, let alone anybody else. Even though they did hurt me, I consider myself the lucky one because I'm getting a second chance here. I win! And when I see them as helpless babies and take into consideration these psychological insights, it is easier for me to rally my empathy and forgive.

The person who hurt you was probably troubled and in great pain himself. You may have been a victim of a victim. You could have been an innocent bystander in the wrong place at the wrong time. You may just have happened to be in someone else's self-destructive path. The more you understand the importance of the twenty choices I'm describing here, the choices to free ourselves from the past, no matter what happened to us, the easier it becomes to forgive. You forgive for yourself—you forgive so that you can move on.

Jesus Christ died publicly, nailed to a wooden cross, sacrificing himself and asking God the Father to forgive the sins of all of us. He even forgave his crucifiers: "Father, forgive them, for they know not what they do" (Luke 23:34). Kind of makes our reluctance to forgive seem pretty stinkin' petty, doesn't it? Jesus is my mentor, and I strive to practice what practical parables he taught.

Here's another reason to let loose our grudges—scripture says, "For if you forgive men their trespasses, your heavenly Father will also forgive you" (Matthew 6:14). I don't know about you, but I know I need to be forgiven. Forgiveness acknowledges that we can trust in a larger guidance system that also levies the ultimate justice. That's just icing on the cake.

Psychotherapist Robin Casarjian uses the following excerpt from a *Time* magazine article in her forgiveness workshops: "The psychological case for forgiveness is overwhelmingly persuasive. Not to forgive is to be imprisoned by the past, by old grievances that do not permit your life to proceed with new business. Not to forgive is to yield oneself to another's control. If one does not forgive, then one is controlled and locked into a sequence of actions, a response of outrage and revenge. The present is overwhelmed and devoured by the past. Those who do not forgive are those who are the least capable of changing the circumstances of their lives. In this sense, forgiveness is a shrewd and practical strategy for a person or a nation to pursue. For forgiveness frees the forgiver." Whether we need to forgive ourselves or others—or both—forgiveness allows us to exorcise the demons from the past. Our vision of the future is bright.

I will not permit any man to narrow and degrade my soul by making me hate him. —BOOKER T. WASHINGTON

Steps to Self-Forgiveness

Often, in doing work on ourselves, we come to realize that the person we most need to forgive is ourselves. I was much harder mentally on myself than on anyone else. If this is true for you as well, try Joan Borysenko's steps toward self-forgiveness:

1   Recognize what you're responsible for and holding on to.

2   Confess your story to another person and to God, as in the rite of confession in church, or in silent prayer.

3   Consider what specific action needs to be taken to resolve things with the other person, if needed. (In the Judd family, we sometimes go together to our therapist, who acts as a mediator. We all feel we're on safe ground and in a meeting dedicated to finding a solution.)

4   Reflect on what you have learned. Self-forgiveness opens you up to more opportunities for continued positive growth. We also discover hidden talents for healing we had no idea existed within us.

5   Realize that anger is biologically toxic and can make you ill.

6   Continually look to God for help.

The more you know yourself, the more you can forgive yourself. —CONFUCIUS

Forgiving Others

No matter who we are or what our personal story is, there comes a time in the process of seeking to heal our hearts that we must forgive those who have wounded us. For only the act of forgiveness can move us out of the victim stance and free us to leave the past behind. Depending on the wounds you've suffered, this might involve deep psychological and spiritual work. No one can do it for you or talk you into it. Only you can know when you are ready.

If you're stuck in resentment and forgiveness is proving difficult, one way to begin is described by M. J. Ryan in her book *Attitudes of Gratitude:* "What helps the forgiveness process is to understand that resentment is a second-hand emotion, a cover for underlying feelings that have never been expressed. That's why it is useful to do a practice called 'A Damage Report.' In a letter (that you never send) to your abuser, write down all the effects the wounding had on you, in as much detail as you possibly can. Don't hold back. Then create a boundary, something like: I will get up and leave the room if someone is verbally abusing me; or I will not stay with anyone who is abusing drugs. This will help you develop trust that you will protect yourself against such circumstances and people in the future. Then write a note of forgiveness to yourself for not having stated your boundary before and a note of thanks to the other person for the learning, so that it won't happen again."

If you fully express your pain and create the boundary, forgiveness will more easily flow, for you know you won't allow yourself to be mistreated like that again. Bury the hatchet and forget where.

There are many ways to victimize people. One way is to convince them they are victims. —KAREN HWANG

The Power of Compassion

Learning to forgive ourselves and others is a breakthrough because it allows us to open up and become more compassionate. The state of our health and happiness depends on the healing power of compassion. So if you've been harboring anger against yourself or someone else, beware of emotional and spiritual heart disease. Your sense of loneliness, alienation, isolation, and depression can kill you. Bet you never thought of it in those heavy terms, did you?

A Buddhist meditation practice called *metta,* or loving-kindness, helps us to develop this compassion and strengthen our desire to forgive. It involves feeling loving-kindness toward yourself and then visualizing your loved ones and extending the loving-kindness toward them. Expansiveness continues to embrace even those you once regarded as adversaries. The good news is that each time you forgive, it gets a little easier to send loving wishes and comfort to others.

Here is Joan Borysenko's version of *metta* that Ashley taught me:

May I be at peace.

May my heart remain open.

May I awaken to the light of my own true nature.

May I be healed.

May I be the source of healing for others.

There is nothing noble about being superior to some other man.
The nobility is in being superior to your previous self.

—HINDU PROVERB

Your Turn Now

How are anger and resentment from your past causing you to disconnect from yourself and others? Have you built up some emotional scar tissue? Don't pout, let it out. That was then and this is now. Have the good judgment to forgive yourself and others! Once you forgive past misdeeds, you'll stop thinking and behaving like a wounded child, and then can reclaim your authentic power as an adult.

Forgiveness is the quicker picker-upper. Once we've 'fessed up to a misdeed and have made amends, it's time to take off the handcuffs and turn ourselves loose! As you allow forgiveness to free you, you begin to really celebrate the best the rest of life has to offer you.

So next time you make a mess, don't sweep it under the rug. Don't cover it up, clean it up—using the techniques I suggested in this chapter. Just as you'd use a paper towel on a spill, clean it up and then throw it away. But don't forget to apologize if needed. Shame is attaching yourself to the guilt so much that you believe you are the mistake. "I'm sorry" is cathartic for both offender and offendee. In a study of medical malpractice, it was discovered that 37 percent of litigants would never have sued if they'd gotten a complete explanation or an apology. I've discovered that there are four parts to an effective apology:

1   Admit your mistake without excuses.

2   Confess you feel bad about the consequences of your act.

3   Be sincere and mean it.

4   Make sure you don't do it again.

In addition to the practices of forgiveness I suggest here, try this visualization when you feel weighed down by anger or resentment:

> *Identify the grudges you currently have toward others and vizualize each as a heavy brick. Load these symbolic bricks into a backpack you strap on your back for a climb up a mountain. (A mountain represents a higher consciousness where you'll be rewarded with freedom and peace of mind.)*
>
> *As you slowly begin to climb, you realize you can't make progress with these weights piled upon your back. As you throw out each specific grievance brick, envision it falling beneath you until it disappears completely from view. Or picture yourself handing it back over to the offender—or throwing it at them, if you must. Just know it's not yours any longer.*
>
> *Continue moving forward and upward until all your burdens are gone. As you hit the peak, you feel lighter and proud of yourself. From your broad vantage point, you can now see clearly in all directions.*
>
> *Ahhhhh . . .*

Doesn't it feel great? In the words of the old spiritual quoted by Martin Luther King, Jr., in his "I Have a Dream" speech: "Free at last, free at last. Thank God Almighty, we're free at last."

Neither a lofty degree of intelligence, nor imagination, nor both together go to the making of a genius. Love! Love! Love! That is the soul of a genius. —Wolfgang Amadeus Mozart

9 Your Strengths and Passions Are the Essence of Your Happiness

This is the story of how I got my "kicks on Route 66" and discovered Choice #9: YOUR STRENGTHS AND PASSIONS ARE THE ESSENCE OF YOUR HAPPINESS. On the long cross-country drive from California to Kentucky to attend nursing school, I had plenty of time to think. Because I had spent time figuring out how my beliefs, based on memories and past experiences, had been influencing my choices, I was now free to begin living out my values—what was important to me, what I truly wanted. On the open road, I opened my mind to this new set of questions.

On Route 66, my future was an exciting destination. Enjoying the changes of scenery, I had the realization that all my dissatisfactions with my life were rooted in my weaknesses. I wasn't good at being a waitress because I wanted to sit down and talk to customers. I wasn't good as a clerk because there was no time for interaction. I resented selling products if I didn't believe in them. Neither was I good as a receptionist, since people just passed me by. My least favorite gig had been a short stint as a model, even though it paid the most. I didn't care that much about looking good. I want to *do* good.

At first, while watching for the right turnoff, I kept going through the litany of things that turned me off. Soon, however, I began looking out for signs of what I *did* want. I may have been following a map to Kentucky, but I was revising my personal map to happiness at the same time. My internal landscape was changing as I traveled.

Psychological studies have found that our jobs are most satisfying when the task more closely matches our abilities. So if the dissatisfaction I felt in my previous jobs was based on the restrictions of not having enough personal contact, then finding a job that allowed more interaction and use of my people skills became a goal. As I drove through the vast desert expanses of Nevada and New Mexico, I opened up to allow various scenarios to play out in my mind.

By the time I reached Kentucky, the silence had allowed divine wisdom to get through to me. I began to understand what I was good at. I saw that one of my talents is empathy. I am able to pick up on the feelings and thoughts of others. This talent is one of my strengths. It is also one of my passions. (Strengths and passions usually go hand in hand, as you will discover as you read on.) Hmmmm . . . nursing was not only a good way to earn a stable income (the reason I thought I had chosen it), but also a wonderful way to take my heart to work and use my empathy to help others.

Recognizing that I should concentrate on my strengths and passions was a breakthrough moment for me, just like the breakthrough that helped me to look in the Mirror of Truth and see new choices, or to recognize that I would be happier if I forgave. Exploring strengths and passions would allow me to stop focusing on what was wrong in my life and begin moving toward what I loved.

Nursing was indeed personally satisfying. As a people lover, I worked well in a team and one-on-one with my patients. Because of my sincerity, I found it easy to build trust. After my shifts at the hospital, as grueling and nerve-racking as they might have been, I went to sleep feeling good about myself. The unexpected discovery was that I function well in high-stress and emergency situations.

Once I began to build my life around my strengths, I realized I was actually using them no matter what I was doing. When later I got into singing professionally with Wynnona, it was easy for me to sing harmony because I was empathizing with her feelings and emotionality. I was enhancing her best efforts. Singing is a product of another of my talents: communication, whether writing the song or singing it. In combination, empathy and communication allow me to give voice to others' perspectives and circumstances in song. And I am using both of those strengths now in writing this book because I care about how you feel and hope to give you ideas on how to enjoy your life more. I want to communicate these breakthroughs that changed my life.

Everyone has inside of him a piece of good news. The good news is that you don't know how great you can be! How much you can love! What you can accomplish! And what your potential is!
—ANNE FRANK

Focus on What You Are Good At Already

It frustrates the heck out of me that many people obsess on their weaknesses. I was a voracious learner in school, but I dreaded math. I would get a headache or stomachache before Mr. Anson's geometry class. It seemed an injustice that, although I had predominantly A's and B's on my report card, Daddy punished me for the C in math. Instead of celebrating my earnestness to excel in all other subjects, I dreaded handing him my report card every six weeks. I tried being tutored and applied myself to the fullest extent I was capable of. Yet I couldn't achieve above a C in geometry. Through the years I've happily shrugged off my inability to perform mathematical problems. Ha, ha, today I feel vindicated, because new brain research proves that we should not focus on damage repair, but instead should turn our attention toward our strengths. (P.S. Mr. Anson, now I hire an accountant.)

Researchers say that when we are born, all the neural pathways in our brains are firing. But by the time we are adults, certain pathways have been more highly developed through use (those are our strengths). Connections to others that we don't use (our weaknesses) actually begin to break. Training in our weaknesses might make us able to do something a little better than before, but it will never come easily. Therefore we will never be excellent at it or love doing it.

Talent is the raw material of what comes naturally to you. We're all born genetically programmed with propensities toward certain talents. Each time your brain experiences a use of your talent, the synaptic connections are strengthened even more. That's why each of us has the capacity to be excellent at certain things and not at others.

Our strengths are ways of thinking that we love to follow—we've followed them so often that they have carved deep grooves in our brains. Now they come easily to us; we can't help but follow them. And the more we know what they are, the more we can use them on purpose to follow our dreams.

If at first you don't succeed, try again, then quit.
There is no point in making a fool of yourself. —W. C. FIELDS

Use Strengths to Overshadow Weaknesses

The more we clarify what our strengths are, the more we can employ them to outweigh our weaknesses. Wy was one of the lucky ones who discovered her talent early. She was only twelve when she uncovered her gift for and love of music. Her admitted weakness was an inability to contain her emotions and express herself comfortably in conversation. Instead of spending her life beating herself up about her shortcomings, she turned all of her attention to her extraordinary musical talent. After all, music expresses emotions that words can't even define! By training in her talent, she found a way to channel and release her feelings. It's brought her great fulfillment and success (as well as enjoyment for the rest of us).

Wy's been able to detour around other weaknesses as well. She wasn't able to sit still long enough to learn music theory or to endure traditional music lessons. However, by hanging out with other musicians, observing, asking questions, and learning on the spot, she practiced discipleship. There are many ways to learn.

Eight-year-old Ashley, too, found her talent early and capitalized on her strengths. She exhibited an obvious attraction to literature, and particularly the acting out of stories. Like a moth to a flame, she's always been drawn to dramatic storytelling. My little drama aficionado had imaginary playmates, read incessantly, went to good movies, and invented plays and skits.

You and I can sidestep the areas in which we don't excel. I now delegate tasks to others or figure out how to use a talent to work around a weakness. For instance, I loathe meetings. So I've figured out to (1) make a list of goals, (2) send my questions, problems, and possible solutions to the attending members in advance, (3) set a time limit for my participation in the meeting, and (4) request that business that doesn't need my input happen after I leave. Also, (5) I even carry a pick-me-up aromatherapy vial of lavender in my purse to apply at pulse points when I start to get distracted. I take along some mints and always sit where I can see out a window.

The greatest gift of a lifetime is being exactly who you are.
—JOSEPH CAMPBELL

To Each His Zone

Your strengths and passions are very closely linked. Your strengths are ways of thinking that you bring to a given situation. Your passions—what you love to do—are the outlets for these strengths. Our strengths underlie our passions—no matter what we are doing, we're using them. So in my case, I am passionate about the ways people heal, about music, and about writing. In all three of these, I put to use my talents of empathy and communication. I may develop other passions as I'm exposed to more issues, but my innate strengths still remain the same.

From a biochemical standpoint, your brain is a drugstore of neurochemicals. When your mind directs the brain to put your talents to use through your passions, these feel-good neurochemicals flow throughout your body. They bind at receptor sites on your organ systems. Hence the term "being in the flow." You literally go into a zone and lose track of time. This is when your life is as you always thought it could be! You are energized by what you're doing, so you want to do it again. You not only feel happier, but your immune system is improved. This means better health in spirit, mind, and body.

Someone once said, "A life without passion is like dressing up a corpse." So true! Because of the release of these good biochemicals, our passions give us the energy to act. The more passion we have for a project, the more fun we have along the way. And the more likely we are to succeed!

I recently visited my friends in the group U2 in their studio in Dublin, Ireland. As I watched them recording, I saw how lead singer Bono is a perfect example of a person who works from his strengths and passions. He writes, sings, and performs. He is also passionate about social activism and uses his public platform to reach out to others. Ashley and Wy spent time with Bono sounding the alarm that one out of five people in the continent of Africa is infected with HIV. Bono told me that even when he appears in front of millions of people, he doesn't get nervous. We agree that it's not about us personally—we're representatives for people with no voice.

As is true of Bono and a lot of my pals who are social activists, figuring out your passions helps you make commitments. Then you get motivated to act. Once you experience the rewards of working from your strengths and passions, you're excited about moving onward. The law of physics states that bodies at rest tend to stay at rest, bodies in motion tend to stay in motion. Our passions set us in motion.

My father always told me, "Find a job you love and you'll never have to work a day in your life." —JIM FOX

Follow Your Bliss

Tommy Waller is a jovial farmer who sells his organic vegetables and his wife Sherri's homemade jams, jellies, and baked goods out in front of a small grocery store in our village. One hot afternoon while chatting as he was weighing some fresh-picked tomatoes, I discovered Tommy's previous life. He had been an officer with Federal Express. He and his wife had been part of the briefcases, nice-cars, and big-home set—until one day they'd had a breakthrough and realized they were not living their passion. Their passion was family, connecting with nature, and a simpler, more rewarding daily life. They now live contentedly with their six children on a farm, with no TV, telephone, fax, e-mail, or computer. In the admonition of Joseph Campbell, they "followed their bliss" and found a more satisfying life. They practice voluntary simplicity so they have less to take care of and keep up with.

Another person I've met who knows that less is more is neuroscientist Margaret Grade, Ph.D. She left the world of academia to be the chef at Manka's Lodge in Inverness, California. There is no menu at Manka's Lodge. The food they serve is whatever has been caught or pulled from the earth, or fresh game from the immediate area. Margaret kayaks to work. Over dinner there recently, she described the "Mushroom Man," a local farmer who pulls his jalopy truck up behind their kitchen every afternoon to deliver the mushrooms he has picked that day. He will not accept pay for doing what he loves.

As a medical scientist, Margaret knows enough about the mind-body-spirit connection to recognize the documented connection between job satisfaction and health. Margaret chose to change careers. If you are not currently passionate about your work, you risk illness. Job dissatisfaction is a better predictor of heart attack and disease than high blood pressure, obesity, or even smoking. So when you follow your passions, you preserve or enhance your physical well-being.

The man that says it can't be done counts the risk, not the reward.
—ELBERT HUBBARD

Your Turn Now

Are you making a living, or are you making a dying? To find out, let's turn our attention to identifying your strengths and passions.

Research shows that each of us has five core strengths. These are talents you can't learn in school, by watching someone else, or through a book. They come from self-awareness through the practices I encourage here. That's not to say that you have to be perfect at every facet of activity for something to be a strength. It does mean, however, that you should focus on following this potential to its fullest.

- What do you consider your strengths right now?

- What comes easily for you? What do you do pretty predictably well, even skipping certain steps?

- What are you drawn to do?

- What makes your heart sing?

- What do you get recognized and validated for?

- What has always seemed to come naturally to you?

- What do you resent doing? How can you delegate this task or minimize your participation in it?

- Are you more comfortable when interacting with others, or do you prefer to work alone?

- When you were a child, what did you think you'd be?

- Are you right-brained (creative, expressive, musical), as Wynonna, Ashley, and I are, or are you left-brained (rational, mathematical, and logistical)?

If identifying your strengths is difficult for you, you might want to take a look at the book *Now, Discover Your Strengths,* by Marcus Buckingham and Donald O. Clifton. It offers ways to figure out just what you are good at.

What are your passions? A sure sign is the degree of satisfaction an activity provides. Another is losing track of time when you are doing it, like Ashley when she's acting or Wynonna and me when we're in the studio recording. Make a list of everything you love and feel passionately about. Keep it in a convenient place, such as on the coffee table by the TV, on the kitchen table, or in the bathroom. Add to it every time you discover you're enjoying yourself.

Once you identify your strengths and passions, build your life around them every way you can. Don't become an expert in trying to correct your weaknesses any longer. Shift your focus from weak areas to relishing and building on your strong areas. Identifying what you love and are good at is powerful knowledge to help you move forward along that path to who you are meant to be.

10 Intuition Is Your Secret Guidance System

Rocking in a chair on the front porch of our remote house on a mountaintop in Kentucky shortly after we arrived to begin our new life, I was watching a summer storm move in. Along with the flash of lightning, I had a major "aha" flash that led me to the importance of Choice #10: INTUITION IS YOUR SECRET GUIDANCE SYSTEM. No one in my family or circle of friends had ever even spoken the word "intuition." However, as I sat alone that dark night listening to the sounds of silence in that lush natural setting, I realized that my intuitive knowing had become my guiding force. In the past, I had let circumstances and other people control my life. Everything began to shift for the better once I woke up to the truth that I could make choices based not on what others wanted but on my own inner wisdom.

That night back in Hollywood when my psycho boyfriend beat me and the startlingly grotesque visual in the Mirror of Truth forced me to go deeper, I had begun the process of turning inward. Once I began exploring my feelings, intuition began subtly nudging me in the right direction. It had guided me to leave California and return to my roots, to get an education and become a nurse, to raise my girls in a family-oriented, natural atmosphere. Thanks to discovering my intuition, I felt at peace on this mountaintop. Ahh . . . it felt so right, I vowed to trust my inner guidance system the rest of my life.

So it was my intuition that led me a few years later to go into the music business with Wy. It was also my intuition that told me Ashley was strong enough to handle Wy's and my touring. It helped me know Larry was the man for me. And when I got sick with hepatitis C and was deciding how to face my grim prognosis, I trusted my intuition for comfort and instruction on how to survive. It prompted me to begin searching on my own for ways to heal—and to write this book.

You must have a room or a certain hour of the day or so where you do not know what was in the morning paper, where you do not know who your friends are, you don't know what you owe anybody, or what they owe you—but a place where you can simply experience and bring forth what you are and what you might be. . . . At first you may find nothing is happening . . . but if you have a sacred place and use it, take advantage of it, something will happen. —JOSEPH CAMPBELL

Follow Your Own North Star

Intuition is our inner knowing, the part of us that serves as an inner compass. Think of it as a North Star to guide us to our destiny. It is one of the most powerful, albeit most underused, resources at our disposal. It's our inner wisdom and is always going to steer us right. It's the one trustworthy source of knowledge and has our best interest at heart.

I've learned about the research on intuition from my friend the neuroanatomist and psychiatrist Mona Lisa Schulz, M.D., Ph.D., who is a recognized expert in intuition. In her book *Awakening Intuition,* she defines it as "the process by which subtle insights come into our senses, minds, bodies and dreams, containing ideas which have no relationship to fact or rational reasoning processes." She says that while you and I are awake, in a dream state, or in a state of consciousness somewhere in between these two states, ideas may flicker across our mind that at first seem quite illogical, nonlinear, impractical, and unrelated to any of our past experiences.

That is certainly true of all the decisions I make based on my intuition—there are all kinds of logical, rational reasons for me to make other choices. Yet over and over again, even in the life-or-death situation of my hepatitis C diagnosis, I chose to follow my inner voice over "logical" advice like "Go home to bed and rest." That's because I know in the very fiber of my being that intuition is the language through which divine consciousness speaks to each human being. I encourage you to allow yours to speak to you.

Intuition is our sixth sense. It allows us to perceive or sense outside of the range of our usual five senses (vision, hearing, smell, taste, body sensations) to greatly widen our doors of knowing. The intuition network consists of the brain, dreams, and the body. It uses the body to send messages of a sense of well-being, foreboding, pain, or disease.

The value of this "language" created by our brain and bodies allows us to gain perception, insight, understanding, and compassion about our past and to make decisions about the future. Intuition can assist us emotionally, physically, and spiritually. It can help us decide if a person, job, move, or treatment is right for us, despite what anyone else is saying. Intuition can also help us create *synergy* in our lives. Synergy is the simultaneous doing of two things that has a greater impact than the sum of the individual effects. The word comes from two Greek words: *syn,* which means "together," and *ergon,* which means "work." When you look to make a change, synergy maximizes the impact of your efforts, and intuition can help guide you as to which actions will have such an effect.

Intuition comes in various forms. *Clairvoyance* refers to intuitive thoughts that come true in the future. *Premonitions* are thoughts about something or someone that may come true tomorrow or soon. *Coincidence* is God's way of staying invisible. Wy, Ash, and I see the invisible world. When something strikes us as a spiritual insight, we refer to it as a "God wink." *Synchronicity* is two events coming together with a specific message for you. The more you notice them, the more they will appear. So start looking for signs and symbols.

Freud believed our subconscious speaks to us through intuition, dreams, and slips of the tongue (known, of course, as "Freudian slips"). Carl Jung, his onetime disciple, believed that "dreams are a little hidden door into the innermost and most secret messages of the soul." Pay attention to powerful, vivid, and recurring dreams as well as the whispers of intuition during the day.

A girlfriend who's a psychiatrist at UCLA, Dr. Judith Orloff, specializes in intuition. Judith believes that "the future of medicine lies in reincorporating intuition and spirituality—vital parts of our wisdom usually disenfranchised from health care. With intuitive healing, every aspect of one's being gains a vote in the search for well-being, opening the door to total health—of our bodies, our emotions, and our sexuality." Judith calls me an "empathic intuitive," meaning that I sense other people's problems. I sense them viscerally and pick up visual clues as well as

Solitude first allows me to empty my mind of all the needless worry about others' needs; it then slowly but consciously lets me fill up that space with my inner knowing. This is when my best ideas come to me. Solitude is creativity's best friend. Things start occurring that I hadn't previously thought of or recognized.

I found I had less and less to say, until finally, I became silent, and began to listen. I discovered in the silence the voice of God.
—SØREN KIERKEGAARD

Do Not Disturb

My need for solitude every morning is legendary among our organization. The word "soliloquy" is related to "solitude" and means to talk to oneself about innermost thoughts, in privacy. On tour one day, I was enjoying an early morning soliloquy as our bus pulled into a hotel. When our road manager checked in at the front desk, a phone message waiting for him read: "From Martha—her mother passed away. Please tell Naomi." A friend's mom had died, and she needed someone to talk to. However, our road manager misread the note, thinking instead that it was my mother who had passed away. He was badly shaken about being the one to deliver such tragic news.

After the confusion was cleared up, he jokingly said that the predicament had posed a double dilemma for him. He was dreading having to waken me and disturb my privacy almost as much as he was dreading telling me my mother had died.

Don't Just Sit There, Do Nothing

Taking time for your intuition is not easy. Today's culture is obsessed with doing, busyness, and producing. It shows little value for allowing us to just be who we are—a human being instead of a human doing.

Ashley, Wynonna, and I were lounging in my kitchen one evening, filling out a psychological quiz in a magazine. One of the questions was "When you have spare time, how do you like to spend it?" Ashley's response was that she would peruse any new movie scripts being offered her. Her answer revealed that Ashley values pursuing her passion for acting. My response was that I use spare time writing correspondence to friends. This revealed that I value nurturing and bonding. Then Wynonna languidly drawled, "When I have spare time, I like to waste it." Ashley and I chuckled at Wy's balanced perspective. Her response proved she values freedom and space. How do you spend your spare time? Wy says to tell you to give yourself permission to do nothing.

Within us there is a stillness and a sanctuary to which
we can retreat at any time and be ourselves by learning to do . . .
nothing. —ANONYMOUS

Your Turn Now

Society honors productivity. I inherited a belief from my dad about the importance of hard work. I still sometimes fight a nagging feeling that I should be doing something productive. Check in with yourself now about your beliefs regarding productivity:

- Do you struggle with a persistent feeling that you should be busy all the time?

- Do you have a place (favorite chair, porch swing, hammock, backyard) for quiet breaks?

- To what degree do you feel your innate value is based on your output?

- Do you think you're still lovable and have worth even when you're not doing something?

Starting tomorrow morning, choose to take twenty minutes to be silent within before you go out into the noisy world. If you are off and running in the morning, trying to get a decent breakfast on the table for your family, taking kids to school, or rushing to work, and don't have the time for solitude, plan to go to bed a half hour earlier and get up a half hour earlier. Let your family know that this privacy is something that is not optional. You'll be setting a good example for them about the importance of everyone having quiet time.

One definition of solitude is "the absence of human activity." Solitude is refreshment for your soul that allows time for the small voice of your inner knowing to be heard. Let solitude be your classroom for learning from your intuition.

In solitude, you will hear your intuition whispering volumes of information to you. Intuition involves those subtle, nudging hints that let you know when a person is not who he's putting himself up to be. It lets you know whether to take that job, whether it's time to have a baby, whether your spouse is faithful or not. It allows a panoply of subtle clues to float through your subconscious mind and then register onto your conscious mind.

Walking in my valley, Dr. Mona Lisa Schulz taught me about *ancestral memory*—our universal, shared subconscious, as well as wisdom that is transmitted genetically. Here's a practice to access this storehouse of accrued wisdom as well as your own personal intuitive knowledge:

1   Begin by eliminating outside stimuli, noise, and distractions.

2   Get comfy. Breathe deeply and slowly.

3   Ask a question you want guidance on rather than stating the problem. For instance, "How should I respond to Fred?" is better than "I have a problem with Fred." The intuitive mind loves questions, and the more you refine your question, the better. Remember, a well-posed question is half the answer.

4   Sit quietly and allow whatever images (an image can be a picture, a sound, or a feeling) to flash across the screen of your mind. Be open to what emerges—don't judge what comes up as good or bad.

5   Realize that intuition is nonlinear. It is associative; it makes connections between things that aren't necessarily logical. Whatever comes up, ask yourself, "How is this true for me? What could this have to do with me right now?" For instance, if you can't get a song out of your head, rather than considering that a distraction, think about whether the lyrics are the message.

6   Thank your intuition for its help. The more you appreciate what you receive, the more you will receive.

There's no one right way. For some people, walking slowly, opening to messages, works best. For others, closing their eyes or writing is better. Feel free to explore what is most effective for you.

Your life won't change just from tapping into your inner wisdom. Like me, you must learn to act on your intuitive hits with abandon. And that's where Choice #11 comes in!

And the day came when the risk to remain tight in a
bud was more painful than the risk it took to blossom.

—ANAÏS NIN

11 Risk Allows You to Become Who You Were Meant to Be

Maybe you've heard the saying that life gives us the test first and the lessons later. At this point in my life, in my mid-thirties, putting myself through nursing school, I'd survived lots of tough tests and learned the lessons from Choices 1 to 10. I knew for sure that peace of mind is the goal and that change is the true nature of our world. I'd learned to first question everything and explore my choices. I committed to reversing any curse. I could see clearly now through informed eyes what was standing in my way. Becoming a detective had helped me tremendously as I discovered how my early family dynamics had been influencing me. I'd been surprised by the benefits of forgiveness. I was building my life around my strengths and passions. Accessing my intuition was now an essential part of my everyday search for guidance and wisdom. Now I was eager to put all this self-knowledge into practice. If life is a schoolroom, it was graduation time!

To get to this point on my path, I'd taken some risks. But to really be all I could be, I would have to take even more. There was no turning back now. I had to embrace risk, knowing deep in my bones Choice #11: RISK ALLOWS YOU TO BECOME WHO YOU WERE MEANT TO BE.

It had been a humungous risk transporting Wynonna and Ashley from Hollywood to bare-bones Appalachia, away from their friends to a remote mountaintop. I was adamant about living without a TV or telephone. They were not amused. They considered it child abuse and teasingly threatened to report me. But because I'd chosen to take this risk, we were all three soon to discover who we were meant to be.

One languid night, searching for some way to pass the time, I handed Wynonna a cheap plastic guitar someone had given me. I still recall my poetic introductory words, "Do not break this over my head." There was an immediate flash of recognition, as if she had been reunited with some hidden part of herself. It was a God wink!

At the time, our mother-daughter relationship had deteriorated to a chronically combative level. We could barely talk to each other. Wy and I were like two souls longing to fuse but afraid to even touch. Music became the glue holding us together. Singing allowed us to connect in a nonthreatening manner and encourage each other's gifts. We felt cautiously hopeful as we began to build something brand new together. Harmony was the literal and figurative result.

For me personally, there was a glorious relief as a mother: Eureka, Wy's found it, she's going to be OK! But I was bitten by the music bug too. My intuition began alerting me that I could use music to fulfill my own passions to connect with and help others, most of all my own child. I knew singing was Wy's destiny, and my responsibility and desire were to support her. Plus I loved singing with her. It was obviously a passion because it came naturally and I lost track of time. I began writing songs, which became an outlet for the creativity that I'd never known I had. Up until then, my life had been all about grunt work and struggling to survive. Now, while busting up coal for our potbelly stove or doing laundry with our Maytag wringer washer, I hummed melodies. Lyrics floated to the surface of my mind. I would dream up songs and then Wy and I would sing them together.

That magical summer, Ashley, my outgoing, popular, and well-spoken daughter, also found her passion—she discovered reading. Her first books, I believe, were C. S. Lewis's *Chronicles of Narnia*. And so it was that as Wynonna sat for hours hunkered over her guitar on the front porch steps, Ashley sat under the big fairy tree in the front yard, falling head over heels in love with drama.

To this day, she remains the most voracious reader. Literature planted the seeds of imagination in her already fertile mind. Her inner fantasy life blossomed. When the time comes that I'm sitting in the audience at the Oscars, watching Ashley accept her leading-lady Oscar, in my mind's eye I shall remember my little "sweet pea" sitting under the fairy tree, enthralled by her book.

No single event can awaken within us a stranger totally unknown to us. To live is to be slowly born. —ANTOINE DE SAINT-EXUPÉRY

Rhinestones, Big Hair, and Guitars

As Wy and I got more obsessed with music, it became obvious that Nashville, Tennessee, aka Music City U.S.A., was where we needed to be. My family thought I had totally lost it at this point. But I was so jazzed by Wy's talent and the thrill of the big adventure, I was champing at the bit to take the risk.

So in May of 1979, I piled fifteen-year-old Wynonna, eleven-year-old Ashley, and cardboard boxes of all our possessions into a junky car whose primary color was Bondo. We arrived in Nashville with no fanfare and less than two hundred bucks in my old plastic pocketbook. The three of us shared one cheap, funky motel room and ate a lot of bologna and crackers. But that risk and lots of hard work were worth it. The rest of our Cinderella story is the stuff of country music legend.

Then, after eight glorious years of fame and fortune touring as the Judds, the fairy tale ran headlong into a grim reality. My hepatitis C prognosis of less than three years to live forced me to consider the greatest risk of all—life or death. I credit my positive experience with risk taking for setting me up to take the ultimate gamble. Against all advice and all odds, I chose to risk trusting my intuition. I went on the road again, for the Farewell Tour. As I pranced onto the stage every night for the following year, I was taking a big leap of faith. I hoped that performing would be better for my physical, emotional, and spiritual health than lying in bed at home. I hit the jackpot!

Wynonna also had to take a huge risk when it came time for her to go solo. The night she was to perform her first concert alone, tensions ran high at that Texas auditorium. No one spoke as we nervously waited on her bus. Pacing back and forth, she was visibly trembling with fear. I tried to soothe her. "Sweetheart, tonight is about rebirth. Birth is always messy and painful," I reassured her, "but I'm living proof that it is so worth it." As we walked hand in hand into the back of the building, just as we'd done a thousand times before, she clung to me desperately.

The pressure, expectation, and excitement were palpable as we huddled together in the darkness at the back of the stage. As the announcer and musicians revved up her intro, Wy froze with fear. She pleaded in a panicked whisper, "Mommy, please give me your best piece of advice," as if I could wave my magic wand so the next two hours would be successful. In an equally dramatic response, I leaned into her face so she could feel my breath on her cheek and admonished, "Sweet tater, read my perfectly lined lips. Never, never watch sausage being made." With a strange smile, she bounded onto the stage to face a cheering crowd. The night launched her first solo album, which went on to become five times platinum. She cut the psychological cord to me, and a new career was born.

Meanwhile, about this same time back home, another enormous risk was being taken. At our farm in Peaceful Valley, Ashley pulled out of our driveway with a loaded U-Haul hooked on the back of her car. It was major déjà vu, since so much of her childhood had been spent hanging out the window of a U-Haul and asking, "Mommy, where are we going now?" (We spent so much time moving we used to get Christmas cards from U-Haul.) This time, Ash was in the driver's seat, a map in her lap and a sign on the back saying, HOLLYWOOD OR BUST. She had decided to follow her intuition and risk it as an actress. She's now one of the most respected and sought-after leading ladies.

Living is a form of not being sure, not knowing what's next or how. The moment you know how, you begin to die a little. The artist never entirely knows, we guess. We may be wrong, but we take leap after leap in the dark. —AGNES DE MILLE

Each Risk Builds Your Ability to Risk

Risk taking is a funny thing. Each time you risk, it becomes easier to do. That's because each time you go for it, it further reinforces your self-esteem and offers concrete evidence that you can indeed succeed. When Wynonna was learning to do shows without me, she was asked to sing her first hit single, "She Is His Only Need," at the American Music Awards show. Dick Clark and I were backstage, extremely concerned about whether she'd even show up. Performing live in front of all of your peers as well as before millions on network TV requires enormous self-confidence, and Wy was still experimenting with performing on her own.

She showed up. In the dressing room, Larry, Ashley, and I dimmed the lights and said a prayer over her. Then I reminded her of a time in the past when she'd taken a leap of faith. She was probably eight or nine, at the swimming pool in Kentucky. She'd worked up the nerve to go off the high dive. But as she slowly ascended the ladder, her fear increased with each step. By the time she reached the top, her shoulders were up around her ears. I could see she was ready to turn back. Yet when she turned around, the ladder was now full of other swimmers. The only way out was to take that leap. I smiled reassuringly at her from the side of the pool. As always, I let her know I was waiting there to come to her rescue. After Wy took the plunge, she returned to do it over and over the rest of the afternoon.

Recalling a victory in the past helped her prepare for the one now in front of her. Wy performed beautifully at the awards show!

At the same time, Ash risked rejection in Hollywood every time she auditioned. But she held on to her belief in herself, and her risks paid off. Never give up!

The poverty of life without dreams is too horrible to imagine. It is the kind of madness which is the worst. —SYLVIA PLATH

To Find Courage, You Must Follow Your Dreams

A fan who'd come on the bus after a concert to visit once asked how in the world we could go onto a stage under a spotlight and sing our hearts out in front of ten thousand strangers every night and how Ash could perform in front of a camera. Without even having to consider my answer, I blurted out, "I can't not do it. My passion is communicating and I love being with Wy, watching her fulfill her destiny, and I love singing stories I've written. Ash's fulfilling her dream too." In other words, loving what we do makes it possible to go ahead and do it. But when I asked him what he did, the man had a dead-eyed response. In a monotone, he recited his occupation like a label he'd been branded with. It was clear that he was a zombie living a life void of dreams.

That's tragic because when you and I don't know our heart's desire, it's meaningless to take a risk. We need to be risking *toward* something—a dream, a goal, the fulfillment of some heart's desire. That's why, as discussed in Chapter 9, it is so important to discover our passions; otherwise we won't have the motivation to risk change. When we know our deepest dreams, we'll be souped up enough to take chances. We need to visualize the rewards and get excited about them.

A poster child for risk taking is a famous friend who exemplifies what is involved in pursuing our dreams. Salma Hayek is a talented actress I met through Ashley. She's so hilarious that I affectionately call her the Mexican Lucille Ball. Salma worked diligently for seven years to bring to the big screen the dramatic story of artist Frida Kahlo. It was a tedious, uphill battle with financing, studios, and so on. Plus, Frida "was a crippled bisexual with a mustache, married to a fat Communist," Salma said with a laugh. Yet, because Salma recognized her passion, took risks, and worked hard, the movie *Frida* became a critically acclaimed Oscar-winning hit.

Watching Salma shine at the movie's premiere, I almost exploded with pride. It was the same sense I felt the first time I witnessed Wy singing on her own or saw Ashley give a stunning performance on the big screen. It's what happens to me whenever I see the story of the struggling caterpillar that eventually emerges into a beautiful butterfly.

Because this is America, ethnicity, background, gender, and age should not get in the way of following your dreams. My author friend Jean Auel is a living testament to this truth. At age forty, she was the mother of five, divorced, and struggling to make her way in life. Then the notion of writing a novel about a young woman in the Ice Age surfaced in her intuition. To those around her, it made no logical sense. But Jean followed her bliss and took a risk, wearing out a string of typewriters writing and rewriting *The Clan of the Cave Bear*—four drafts. Jean Auel has now sold 34 million copies of her *Clan of the Cave Bear* series. Living well is the best revenge.

The legend of Kentucky's Colonel Sanders throws out age stereotypes. Colonel Sanders was living out of the back of his car, barely eking by, day to day. Because franchising was in its infancy, his plan for a chain of fried chicken restaurants seemed absurd. Yet he remained unshakable in his belief that he could produce the best fried chicken anywhere. Because of Colonel Sanders's risk taking, the rest, as they say, is finger-licking-good history.

You're never too young, either. As a judge on *Star Search,* I'm privileged to be sitting in the front row as kids as young as eight stride confidently onto our stage in front of a huge live audience on a prime-time network TV show seen by 15 million people, asking to be judged on their performance. Could you have done this at their age? When I ask why and how they pull this off, the responses I continually get are "I just love to sing and dance" or "I just knew this was something I had to do to get better." After the show, as I counsel with those who don't win, their satisfaction at having pulled off the risk makes it obvious that it was a life-affirming experience. They've risked following their dreams, gained self-respect, learned from the experience, and had fun. The adults on *Star Search* sometimes leave their day jobs when their appearance confirms they need a career change.

In writing this chapter, I've realized that most of my friends dare to dream. Like attracts like. Most of the folks I hang out with are truly passionate about their dreams and don't let lack of education or training stand in the way. For instance, my buddy Jack Horner is one of the world's most renowned paleontologists. Yet he continually flunked out of school and is dyslexic. Once Jack quit trying to fit into the mold of academia, he unleashed his passion for hunting dinosaurs. The brilliant inventor Dean Kamen wasn't just a poor student; he was a horrible student. But Dean was an inveterate tinkerer and now has improved the world with his many inventions. Dean once told me, "It's a job only if you'd rather be doing something else."

We create in constructive ways or we create in destructive ways; either way, creative energy finds expression. —DAN MILLMAN

It May Not Come Naturally, but You Can Do It

Another Dean, Dean Hamer, chief of gene structure and regulation at the National Cancer Institute, has identified what he calls the "thrill gene." My dashing son-in-law Dario Franchitti, Ashley's husband, definitely has it. A genetic predisposition to taking risks nudges him toward thrill seeking. As a professional cart race car driver, Dario goes up to 230 miles per hour. In 2002, he had three first-place wins; he now races for IRL. But perhaps Dario's biggest risk is not on the racetrack, but marrying into our family. In our clan, crazy is a "relative" term, pun intended. (Our Judd coat of arms goes across the chest and ties in the back.)

Just because you may not have been born with the thrill gene doesn't mean you can't take the risks you need in your life. You don't have to drive a race car, sing onstage at Carnegie Hall, or act on a big screen with Robert De Niro. Following your dreams is about giving creative expression to your unique personality—whatever that may be. Researchers in psychology have proven that risk takers who follow their dreams are happier, more productive, and live longer. Risk attracts other colorful people to you, keeps you moving forward toward your set goals, and allows you to grow. When we choose to risk, we are exhibiting faith in ourselves and our abilities to make our dreams come true.

Far better it is to dare mighty things to win glorious triumphs even though checkered with defeat than to rank with those poor spirits that neither enjoy much nor suffer much because they live in that gray twilight that knows not victory nor defeat.
—THEODORE ROOSEVELT

Your Turn Now

Wynonna, Ashley, and I are having a membership drive for our Dreamchasers' Club. Care to join us? The prerequisites are belief in yourself and knowing your beliefs, values, and dreams. Fill out the following questionnaire:

1   Name a time that you took a risk and pulled it off.

2   What would you attempt if you knew you couldn't fail?

3   What would it take to persuade you to stick your neck out? I call Ash my little giraffe 'cause she's always sticking hers out.

4   Is someone in your life discouraging you from being all that you can be? What could their motivation be? Are they jealous? Is it a matter of the bland leading the bland? Realize it's hard for someone who's not a risk taker to understand. Walk around those people—they'll be applauding later.

Identify one place where you need to take a risk. One way to begin to ask the question is to think about how you might be stuck in a comfort zone. If you put a frog in a pot of water and slowly turn up the heat, the frog will remain in the pot and boil to death. However, if you drop the frog into a pot that's already boiling, it will immediately leap out. Consider for a moment that your present comfort zone is that steadily heating pot. Get out now! Consider W. C. Fields's admonition: "The only difference between a rut and a grave is the dimensions." Could it be you're living your life in boring black-and-white, that horrible gray zone?

To practice risk taking, try these three things today:

1   Do something you've never done before, whether it's trying a new food or taking a different way to work.

2   Say something you've been holding back. Don't wait, because there will never be a perfect time or a perfect circumstance.

3   Explore the other side of a situation. To do this, punctuate your thoughts with "But what if . . . ?" Don't allow yourself to get into a thinking rut.

If you have trouble figuring out what your life dreams are—which are the motivations behind the risks you need to take—consider these questions:

- What do you keep pushing to the background?

- What's a longing of your soul that you have been ignoring?

- Whom do you admire and envy?

Ask your intuition to make you more keenly aware of those yearnings throughout your day. Stay open to God winks. Pay attention to what you're drawn to and pulled toward.

Often our self-concept gets in the way of the risks we need to take in our lives. Do you think of yourself in reductive terms—"No one in my family has ever done that before," "I could never do that, I'm too old, too shy, too uneducated, too [fill in the blank]"? You can change that by looking at your risk profile. The more we see ourselves as capable of risking, the easier it gets. Complete the following statements in regard to your comfort with risk:

- I used to be a person who _____.

- Right now, I am a person who _____.

- I am working on being a person who _____.

Remember, the more experiences you have, the more you open yourself up to the possibilities awaiting you. Risk enables you to feel more alive and joyful. I so encourage you to begin living in Technicolor. The future is *wow!*

The human mind is a slide projector with an infinite retrieval system, and an endlessly cross-referenced subject catalogue. The inner images we show ourselves form our lives, whether as memories, fantasies, dreams or visions. We can direct the mind's eye to our inner world to bring about the creative forces of spirituality and healing in our daily life. —MIKE AND NANCY SAMUELS

12 You've Got to Love That Person in the Mirror

I have always played against type. I was a wife and mother at eighteen, went to college in my early thirties. I was thirty-six when Wy and I signed with RCA, ancient for the music business. I had a huge singing career in my forties, and at fifty became a best-selling author and motivational speaker, at the same time that I was becoming a grandmother. Now, at fifty-seven, I've become a TV personality and entrepreneur. No wonder my kids call me "The Mother of Reinvention." Has your life followed the normal chronological order or been varied like mine?

How could I make such drastic changes and be successful at all of them? Because by my mid-thirties, I had a breakthrough that it's all about being defined from within! I chose not to allow myself to be defined by what others think or say. What makes that possible is Choice #12: YOU'VE GOT TO LOVE THAT PERSON IN THE MIRROR—in other words, cultivate healthy self-esteem. I'd learned to just be myself. Hollywood was so full of people who were influenced by the ever-changing superficial culture or by stereotypes of how they should behave. I realized after I returned home to the natural environment of Kentucky and through studying psychology in nursing school that I wanted to live my own life. To the hilt! And I will never act my chronological age. Care to join me?

When the baby boomer generation turned fifty, *People* magazine's cover featured entertainers hitting the big five-oh mark. I was the only celebrity interviewee who seemed to be celebrating this anniversary. It's because I'm happy I've lived long enough to learn about why I think and behave the way I do. Through trial and error, I know what works for me. Do you?

Oprah invited Diane Sawyer and me, who are the same age, onto her TV show to explain why we're so open about being fulfilled and comfortable in our skin and appreciative of our age. I wholeheartedly concur with lovely Diane, who said that part of the answer was that we've "earned a stronger self-confidence and we're prepared to face whatever comes about." Self-acceptance like this is the first part of self-esteem. You must believe that you're good enough just the way you are. Let's age gratefully!

Because of my solid upbringing, I felt self-accepting. When I got sick with hepatitis C, my self-acceptance took a serious blow. I began seeing a therapist to deal with my prognosis, and it surfaced that much of my self-esteem is based on being able to help others solve their problems. Now I couldn't help anyone. Therapists help you dig back into your formative years to see how you got your beliefs. We came to the conclusion that my need to be a healer had been cemented by my sense of helplessness at my brother Brian's death. Through therapy and some of the exercises in this chapter, I began to revise my beliefs. My self-esteem bloomed again.

Keep a close watch on all you do and think. Stay true to
what is right and God will bless you and use you to help others.
—1 TIMOTHY 4:16

What We Need Now Is Love, Self-Love

To win the keys to my tour bus, can you correctly guess what's the number-one indicator for how long you're going to live and how happy and how successful you'll be? *Clue:* Behavioral scientists say you'll never let yourself have more health, happiness, or success than you feel you deserve. This means that right this minute you're attracting what you're feeling worthy of. So the number-one denominator for your getting all the good stuff in life—health, wealth, good relationships, and even longevity—is self-esteem! Makes sense, doesn't it? So figure out your current self-worth on a scale of one to ten. This chapter is dedicated to helping you increase it. Full esteem ahead!

Self-esteem is a measurement of how well you feel about yourself, how confident and capable you judge yourself. This includes how attractive you think you are. We tend to have a set self-esteem point that is developed early on, based on how our first caretakers met our physical needs and bonded with us emotionally.

Yet self-esteem fluctuates over time. You and I are constantly measuring ourselves against our past successes and achievements. If there's a discrepancy between what we've already done and what we still want to do, or if we don't continue to achieve our goals, then our self-esteem may falter. Happily, if we learn to talk lovingly to ourselves and surround ourselves with people who truly love us, their words and acts of encouragement will eventually sink into our brain and boost our lagging self-esteem. Friends are like elevators. They either take us up or bring us down.

Hanging around with psychologists, I keep hearing the term "internal locus of control." Basically it means an inner core of self-esteem that is hardy. People who possess this are ultimately the masters of their own fate. This is what you and I want. Then there's "external locus of control." People with this have low self-esteem. They see themselves as victims of their circumstances. They allow themselves to be at the mercy of those around them. Because they don't feel they are worthy, they don't take responsibility for their lives. They are stuck in a cycle of feeling out of control and blaming others, which results in further low self-esteem and more external locus of control.

You and I can break the cycle by seeing ourselves as masters of our own fate. By the actions you take and every choice you make, you control, to a great degree, what happens to you. You certainly can control your reactions. As you work on creating high self-esteem and an internal locus of control, you'll soon get more of what you're after in life.

Ever hear that country song "Lookin' for Love in All the Wrong Places"? Before you and I can expect to find love with anyone else, we first have to find it within ourselves. Your relationship with yourself is the most basic and crucial one. So who you choose to fall in love with is literally a reflection of how much you love or do not love yourself. Conflict between you and your partner comes down to a reflection of some conflict still going on within yourself.

Until I figured this out, I was attracting very inappropriate men. Because I hadn't been aware of this, I wasn't living up to my potential and wound up with creeps for boyfriends. Like attracts like. So please pause now and take a long, hard look at everyone you are surrounded by. They are an exterior manifestation of your relationship with yourself.

> *One cannot truly accept others unless one also accepts oneself, and self-acceptance at any level is essential for satisfying relationships.*
> —FRANCES VAUGHAN

What's It Worth to You?

In our Pentecostal church's Sunday morning message, Pastor L. H. Hardwick spoke about how self-esteem affects each of us both individually and collectively. He commented on news reports of random drive-by shootings. Pastor pointed out that the shooters are fatherless teens who have been raised in poverty with no education and have no hope for any happiness in their future. Since they don't even love themselves, they have absolutely no concern for anyone else. No one can give what he doesn't have. Kind of puts "Love thy neighbor as thyself" in a new light, doesn't it?

Self-esteem and social status even affect our hormone levels. I've seen studies on this with fish. Like delinquent teens trying to be tough, the strongest fish that successfully fights off competitors has the best mate and the biggest territory, and winds up having the highest testosterone levels. He ends up wearing colorful scales as well.

The same change occurs in monkeys. When a monkey is the head of his family, his testosterone level goes up and he's more likely to obtain even more territory as well. The opposite also holds true. When monkeys lose power and status, their scrotums and testicles shrink as their testosterone level drops. Oops!

Hormones are powerful chemical messages that affect your organs' health. Socioeconomic status is influenced by education, economics, monetary resources, and real estate. When young criminals' self-esteem is diminished because they're poor, uncared-for, and uneducated, it will ultimately endanger their health. If your self-esteem isn't high, it could be affecting your health as well.

Self-esteem also acts as a buffer that cushions the blows of external situations that cause anxiety and depression. In dealing with hepatitis C, I learned so much about the key role self-esteem plays in providing emotional, mental, and physical protection against anxiety provoked by disease. It's important from your immune system's perspective because low self-esteem causes decreased NK (natural killer) cell activity, which fights germs. Anyone with low self-esteem and a suppressed NK cytotoxicity is more vulnerable to infection, cancer, and other serious disease processes. People with high self-esteem have strong immune systems. For instance, actors who win Oscars live six years longer, on average, than those who don't—more evidence of how positive self-esteem enhances health as well as emotional well-being.

The more we can love ourselves and attend to all of life around us with a loving, open, connected heart . . . the more we can be in a beautiful place. —BROOKE MEDICINE EAGLE

Wish upon a Star

Ultimately, self-esteem is about how well you appreciate and value yourself. Self-love is truly the magic wand that can keep you on the right path, prevent illness from taking hold, and make current problems solvable. If only I could wave my rhinestone scepter and instantly grant you the gifts of health, happiness, and prosperity through high self-esteem!

Those of you who have seen me in concert have witnessed my Glinda the Good Witch persona. I'd suddenly appear high on a stage riser in a fabulous ball gown, wearing a rhinestone crown and carrying a scepter. Gracefully I'd glide to the front of the stage, where I'd sprinkle fairy dust upon the front row.

My Fairy Godmother alter ego sprang from performing ceremonies for sick kids from the Make-A-Wish Foundation. After a concert, on our bus Wy would announce me with much fanfare. Together she and I would act out an elaborate ritual to banish fear. The purpose was to boost the kids' self-esteem. We'd let those kids know that they're loved and valuable, and deserving of healing. "Mekka Lekka Hi, Mekka Lekka Hiney Ho. Fear be gone when we say 'go' . . . *Go!*" Kids can easily suspend disbelief. (I'm really a kid in an adult body.) Imagine me now as your very own Glinda and the exercises in this book as a ritual to banish your fears and make your dreams come true!

As entertainers, but mainly as women, we three Judds strive for *personal excellence* in many spheres. Practicing personal excellence is caring enough about yourself to foster your own unique potential and not let anything or anybody keep you from living up to it.

Change happens not by trying to make yourself change, but by becoming conscious of what's not working. —FRITZ PERLS

Happiness Is the Best Cosmetic

I was reading bedtime stories to Elijah and Grace when the issue of self-esteem struck a chord. Fairy tales often involve a beautiful princess marrying a handsome prince and then, of course, living happily ever after. Witches, villains, and mean stepmothers are always ugly, if not grotesque. That's because one of our primal needs is to be attractive so that we will feel desirable and worthy of someone's love and admiration. Biology wants us to find a mate and reproduce. Scientific research confirms that physical attractiveness enhances your opportunities in all areas, whether it's social status, educational and financial opportunities, or romantic connections.

Although being attractive may have its rewards, you'd be surprised to learn that sometimes the advantage isn't nearly as great as you think. Truth is, it's less about how you look and more about how you feel about your appearance!

Your perception is more powerful than reality—and self-esteem drives your perception of yourself. For example, anorexics aren't really overweight; yet, because their body image seems fat in their perception, they refuse to eat. ("I went shopping with Calista Flockhart. She asked, 'Does this dress make my spinal column look big?' "—Gilbert Gottfried.)

No body's perfect! Dissatisfaction with body image can be a strong risk factor for psychopathology such as anxiety and depression. If you perceive yourself as ugly, it's possible to set yourself up for mental problems even though you're not unattractive. Your body image can even change without any corresponding physical change in your appearance. All of us are dissatisfied with our body in some way. Those with high self-esteem take it in stride. People who are unhappy or depressed tend to negatively distort their body image even further.

Men and women have different definitions of what beauty means. My husband doesn't understand why women get manicures, pierce their ears, or wear stilettos. I think his golf outfit is daffy and ties are absurd. Each culture has a different standard also. As a college student, Ashley was hot-rolling her hair and admiring her nose ring while watching the National Geographic Channel. She was amused at the African tribesmen with their body paint and plates stretching their bottom lips. I found her reaction amusing.

The relationship between your self-esteem and your appearance works both ways. How you look and how much you weigh definitely influence your level of self-esteem. But because your appearance and your weight are products of how you're feeling about yourself, if you do something that makes you feel better about yourself, your appearance will improve. In *The Good Look Book,* Drs. John Hartley and Melvin Elson describe how "the way we look not only influences how others treat us, but also affects our own attitudes, behaviors and accomplishments. If we look in a real mirror, not just the reflection of other people's reactions, and we are satisfied with what we see, then there's a good chance we can handle our daily tasks with confidence." We must not be influenced by the perceptions of others. They're reflecting their own issues onto us.

When you take time out (as you are doing reading this book) to work on understanding how you think so you can feel good about yourself on the inside, it's going to show through on the outside. Your posture, speech, and facial expressions will reflect a happier, inner self-confidence. You can look as good as you choose to feel. The result will be like a magnetic attraction drawing others to you.

As your self-esteem improves, there's a shift so that how you feel on the inside becomes more meaningful than whatever is on the outside. Gravity will always win over any effects of cosmetic surgery. Makeup washes off at the end of each day, but loving yourself is the answer to permanent happiness.

Loving ourselves as we are also helps all of us, for it diminishes harmful stereotypes. The more of us who understand that inner happiness matters much more than external looks, the more there will be a positive shift in our cultural perceptions of beauty. Ridiculous, injurious stereotypes such as "Unattractive people aren't as smart or deserving" or "Attractive people couldn't possibly be brilliant too" limit all of us. Celebrities are notoriously vain, since appearance is an integral part of their profession. Ironically, as they sell images of youth and beauty, they fall smack-dab into the very trap they're part of setting for others.

When you understand that feeling good about yourself is more important than the way you look, you'll want to rearrange your values. Aren't good relationships, financial security, and enjoying the social status you want more important to spend your time and energy on than just how you look? So it's not just the love of beauty, it's the beauty of *loving*—yourself.

"Beauty is truth, truth beauty,"—that is all
Ye know on earth, and all ye need to know.
—John Keats

Searching for the Fountain of Smart

Like beauty, aging is also about perception. Perception is in the eye of the beholder. We are free to change our perceptions. I believe in being the best I can be at every stage of life. I'm a Va Va Boomer!

With aging, as when you are going through any change, it always helps to know you're not alone. Never before in the history of the planet has there been such a demographic blip as the current baby boomer population. Almost 86 million folks are over fifty, at least 40-plus million of whom are female. This generation has revolutionized every phase of life thus far, from birth control to allowing fathers to be in the delivery room, to sports, politics, and the business world. Baby boomers' economic clout is gradually changing the way our society perceives its older citizens. Hooray!

Psychologist Dr. Ross Goldstein, president of Summit Psychological Association in San Francisco, refers to this awakening as "the new midlife" because it reflects the changing standard for good looks and healthier living. He says that what people seem to admire most is the ability to live well, have a good appearance, and achieve maximum results from personal potential. These people act too young to grow old.

Yet America remains backward and unlike any other nation in clinging to false standards of youth and beauty. Other cultures revere the wisdom and experience of age and have realistic standards of what's healthy and attractive. The other day at the grocery store I complimented a lovely eighty-year-old woman who obviously takes care of herself. She teared up because she was so pleased and surprised by the acknowledgment.

Check in with your own reactions to those who are ahead of you chronologically. Do you believe that "older people aren't desirable or even interested in sex"? In fact, 90 percent of married men and women in their sixties and seventies are sexually active. How many friends do you have over sixty? Hopefully, you and I will be in their (corrective) shoes someday. Become sensitive to and aware of ways you can raise society's level of admiration and respect toward aging. One thing to do immediately is to be vocal and celebrate your age instead of denying your years. Acknowledge and share what you've learned by having lived through experiences. Be a mentor to others, especially those younger than you. Point out ridiculous media propaganda and educate others to the harm it causes everyone. Don't support products that play to insecurities and promote unrealistic expectations of youth.

As you grow older, changes in your physical appearance, as well as your mental capacity, are inevitable. Entropy isn't what it used to be! Humor intended. You can't bargain with a calendar, but you can cheerfully focus on identifying the many positive aspects of aging: wisdom, self-assuredness, long-term friendships and relationships. I find I experience living more fully because of a broader perspective. I've come to appreciate how precious life is. (One of my threats to Wy and Ash is to live long enough to be a problem to them in my old age.)

New research challenges many of the false assumptions about aging. For instance, our brain cells undergo constant transformation throughout our lives, and our brains are more changeable than was once thought. The brain's electrical, magnetic, and chemical fields are in constant fluctuation since they reflect our moment-to-moment varied experiences. Even brain anatomy is continually being resculpted as cells come and go. It was welcome news when researchers at Princeton University found evidence that thousands of fresh brain cells are born every day. The more we challenge our minds with new information, ideas, and outlooks, the healthier our brains are! So live and *learn*.

Your biological age correlates better with your psychological age than with your chronological age. Chronological age refers to the time since the day you were born and is measured in years. It may be how you describe your age, but it has the least relevance to your actual appearance or health. Biological age is the measure of how your physical symptoms are functioning. Biological markers are the objects of the standard tests you have when you go to a doctor or hospital—blood pressure, pulse, hormone level, cholesterol level, glucose level, and the like. The most important marker is psychological age: how old you feel.

How old would you be if you didn't know how old you was?

—SATCHEL PAIGE

Your Turn Now

The interesting paradox is that when you and I accept ourselves just the way we are, then we begin to improve. As your self-esteem coach, I'm here to help you realize that you're already worthy. I want you to go ahead and love yourself unconditionally. But you're not going to improve your self-esteem just from reading a book or talking about it. You're going to have to apply the ideas here. You form good habits the same way you've gotten harmful ones—practice. As my farmer neighbor Ralph Meachum says, "My field doesn't get plowed just by turning it over in my mind."

Psychologists say it takes about ten weeks to create a habit. Small steps will make big changes. How does one eat an elephant? One bite at a time. And remember, I'm behind you, supporting you each step of the way.

If you look into the Mirror of Truth, can you sincerely say that you love yourself exactly as you are? Key word: *"exactly."* Make a list of all the qualities you like about yourself and read the list out loud three times to the mirror. To help you come to love who you see in your mirror, say these affirmations out loud daily:

I already am all I need to be.

I can be all I want to be.

I honor the happiness and pride I am experiencing now.

I accept and appreciate the love I receive from others.

I attract total financial security.

I accept new rewarding experiences.

Start loving yourself unconditionally. You're all you've got.

What you're thinking right now is influencing
every aspect of who you are. —DR. GLADYS McGAREY

13 You Become Whatever You Think About All Day

Years ago—long before Wy and I made it big in the music business and Ash became an actress—while doing the supper dishes in our small, wood-frame, run-down house, I predicted to my skeptical teenage girls that someday I would write a number-one song. They erupted into fits of laughter. It ticked me off, so I continued, "OK, go ahead and laugh, but I'm also going to win a Grammy for songwriter of the year!" At the time, it did seem ludicrous. Wy, Ash, and I were still living in poverty. I was worried that our old car, dubbed Hunka Junk, wasn't going to last much longer. I didn't have medical coverage or a credit card. At thirty-six, I felt I didn't have much to show for my life. But I still refused to allow anything to stop me from believing I could become all I wanted to be.

Since then, I've written many number-one songs and won that Grammy for songwriter, as well as five other Grammys. Nobody's laughing anymore. I am convinced that it was my solid belief in myself and a well-thought-out plan that resulted in my success. That moment in the kitchen, when I stated my belief, set into motion Choice #13: YOU BECOME WHATEVER YOU THINK ABOUT ALL DAY. The more I told myself I was going to write a hit and win a Grammy, the more I believed it. Eventually the dream was fulfilled. Yours can be, too.

My experience in the entertainment business continues to show me how people's beliefs (their memories and experiences) create their self-talk. Our internal dialogue has profound effects on our potential to achieve happiness and success. As I travel, I meet many people who came from horrible beginnings who've learned how to talk themselves into successful living. If we choose to focus on what's possible and talk to ourselves about what that success will look and feel like, good things follow. If we choose to dwell on the negative, on all the things that could go wrong, we actually talk ourselves into failing. Once again, our future is our choice. The best way to predict your future is to start visualizing it.

Which kind of self-talk are you currently choosing to program your everyday thoughts, actions, and feelings? The most powerful words in the English language are the ones you choose to say to yourself.

Thinking is only a process of talking to yourself. —Anonymous

---

Saying Is Believing

Words hold the power to get what you want and to help you let go of what you don't. They act like a lever to get hold of your mind-body. Words become the outward manifestation of whatever's going on inside your head. They reflect your inner world to your outer world. Sticks and stones can break your bones and words can break your heart—or heal it. Words can create or destroy.

Then there's the F-word. The F-word indicates anger, hostility, and lack of respect for others. It's nothing short of a verbal assault. Another symptom of America's downgrading, cursing conveys ignorance and laziness. The speakers lose credibility because they either don't know or don't care enough to access their vocabulary to select an appropriate adjective or adverb. Such language also reflects their absence of upbringing and manners. Manners are the oil that keeps the machinery of society running smoothly. If you've been using the F-word or cussing, choose to wash your mind out. Become a social lubricant.

Muhammad Ali surely used the power of the spoken word to his mental and physical advantage. Before his big match against Sonny Liston, he was considered a struggling fighter. The media had pretty much ignored him as a contender. Ali kept declaring himself "The Greatest" over and over. He believed in himself and spoke those words out loud! Those now famous words "I am the greatest" made headlines around the world. Ali's inner belief, reflected outwardly, proved he was a champ. He didn't tell reporters that he was "almost the greatest" or that he was "probably the greatest." Because he told himself he was the greatest, Muhammad Ali will forever be known as "The Greatest."

Once you have given a thought life through speaking it, it's like an arrow released from a bow. Remember, too, that once it's left your tongue, it can never come back. A closed mouth gathers no foot. Your words have power to build you up or tear you down mentally, emotionally, and physically. Begin thinking twice before you speak. Holding your tongue will foster self-respect and impress others.

If you gossip, people won't trust you. That's because they will assume you'll also spread untrue, derogatory things about them behind their back. Even the word "gossip" hisses. Gossip stems from low self-esteem and envy. It's a verbalized form of prejudice. Instead of working on their own issues, gossips tear down someone else, perhaps someone they don't even know. They do it to avoid looking squarely at their own relationships, finances, disappointments, and so forth. By talking about the bad things in another person's life, they don't have to feel the pain of their own. They dissociate from their own pain by immersing themselves voyeuristically in someone else's. From now on, if you have some juicy gossip to tell, raise your hand. Then place it over your mouth.

Lies are also a form of protection against painful self-knowledge. How often do you lie? It's a particularly cumbersome defense and creates more problems for our psyche. If you think you are telling a white lie to spare someone else's feelings, better look into the Mirror of Truth. Such lying actually is selfishness because you won't risk having to deal with someone's displeasure. It creates another falsehood that disconnects us from the truth of who we are. True power comes from authenticity; false power comes out of ego and a need to control. Lying separates us from the possibility of experiencing true intimacy with another. Insisting falsely that "nothing could be further from the truth" means keeping you further from yourself and others. Oh, what a tangled web we weave when first we practice to deceive—ourselves!

My mother says, "Words are the clothes our thoughts wear." The truth is always in fashion. No wonder the tabloids are called "rags." I asked a woman at the newsstand why she was buying a tabloid. She replied, "Because my life is so uneventful and boring." People who have low self-esteem and are self-deceptive are suckers for the tabloids. Conversely, the more the truth becomes a dominant principle of our thoughts and speech, the more we will grow and become happier. It's basically a choice toward self-esteem that results in a positive shift within ourselves and then a ripple effect on the world around us.

In the beginning was the Word. The Word was with God and the Word was God. —JOHN 1:1

I Think, Therefore I Am

You and I have beliefs about everything: our weight, appearance, relationships, intelligence, eating habits, work, parenting skills, and how much money we make. Every negative pattern we're engaged in is a result of our own self-limiting beliefs and negative self-talk. Rather than saying to yourself, "I'm the greatest," do you say to yourself, "I don't matter," "She's so much more clever," "I can't hold my own in an argument," or "I can't face their disapproval"? We all have subtle ways of talking negatively to ourselves. Researchers say that 75 percent of our self-conversations are negative. People who engage in negative self-talk drag their spirits and immune systems down. Positive change can't occur if we think things like the following:

Just my luck.

I never know what to say.

I don't know.

I don't have enough talent.

That's impossible.

I am so stupid.

I'm too old.

I can't stop smoking.

I never have enough time.

Everything I eat goes right to my hips.

Today just isn't my day.

No one in my family's ever done that.

I don't deserve it.

It's not my time.

They're all against me.

Nobody gives me a fair shake.

They know stuff I don't.

Negative self-talk is verbal self-abuse. It tempts us to settle for those extra thirty pounds, stay in a dead-end affair, accept failures, or require anger, high drama, or even abuse to be stimulated and feel alive. But you can change the way you are thinking and talking about your life this minute. Your beliefs are the results of your experience. Once you tell yourself you're going to have a better experience, your attitude shifts accordingly. You actually begin attracting better experiences.

Gloom, despair and agony on me. Deep, dark depression, excessive misery. If it weren't for bad luck, I'd have no luck at all.
—HEE HAW DITTY

Believing Makes It So

Researcher Ellen Idler conducted a long-term study on how attitude can influence how long a person lives. Her evidence suggests that our mental outlook is more reliable in gauging longevity than cancer, diabetes, high blood pressure, or even heart disease. That's amazing. The Rutgers University investigation concluded that a woman who considers herself to be in good health is likely to live longer than another woman who may be in similar physical shape but considers herself to be in poor health. Begin adding life to your years by adding positive thoughts and words.

One in four people is born with a brain that is hardwired for thinking positively about himself and his life. We call those lucky folks optimists. However, the rest of us can choose to build a better self-talk system. Optimists understand the broad benefits of positive thinking on mind, body, and spirit. They're set on accentuating the positive and eliminating the negative in themselves and everyone else.

Know anybody in the Piss 'n' Moan Club? I know a hunk who's drop-dead gorgeous, but the guy is humor impaired. Being a "humor being," I shun the stud. However, Gloomy Gus works with a short, balding fellow who has the sunniest disposition. Happy-Go-Lucky has a wonderful smile and radiates warmth and good energy. We glow together (along with everyone in our vicinity).

It's well documented that optimists live longer, are happier, more successful, and more popular than their pessimistic counterparts. A recent Mayo Clinic study found that pessimists have a 19 percent greater likelihood of premature death than optimists. An apple a day may keep the doctor away, but optimists live longer. Optimists are flexible and resilient in their relationships and jobs no matter what problems come up. Ever see one of those "Weebles wobble but they don't fall down" toys? No matter how hard you knock them, they pop back up. That's an optimist. I hope you'll refuse to stay down when you fall, because you *are* going to fall. We all do—it's part of life.

Optimists have figured out that a bad day doesn't constitute a bad life. An unpleasant event is only temporary. It came from a random event meant to teach something or an unskilled choice we have made. That's a lesson I've had to learn, because the entertainment world is a roller coaster of highs and lows. I've had to become skilled at putting things in perspective. It really is all small stuff. Keep asking yourself, "Does this glitch really matter in the overall scheme? Will I even remember it a year from now?"

Most successful people are creative optimists. Babe Ruth, one of the world's greatest baseball players, struck out 1,330 times. Basketball star Michael Jordan was cut from his high school basketball team. Both continued to talk positively to themselves despite their failures—and look what happened!

A person with positive expectations naturally counts on something great happening. Psychologists call this *reframing*. Reframing requires you to put a potentially bad situation into its proper perspective. In the book of Samuel, the Israelite army freaked out when they saw the giant Goliath. They figured the situation was hopeless. But optimistic David with his slingshot and stones thought: "Gee, he's so huge a target, how can I miss?"

Creating positive expectations is a habit you can start developing right now, much in the same way you choose to improve your situation through an exercise routine or diet. As soon as I begin to wake up on my pillow every morning, I say, "Good morning, God." Some people groan, "Ugh, good God, it's morning!" (Maybe they consider "good morning" an oxymoron.) But there is no wrong side of the bed—it's all in your head.

Most people are about as happy as they make up their mind to be.
—ABRAHAM LINCOLN

Self-Made Genius

Why are optimists able to maintain better relationships and succeed better at work than pessimists? Two words: *emotional intelligence*. Optimists are emotionally intelligent. In 1990, the term "emotional intelligence" was coined by psychologists Peter Salovey at Yale and John Mayer at the University of New Hampshire. Emotional quotient (EQ) isn't the opposite of your intelligence quotient (IQ). Some people are lucky enough to be high in both. But while IQ counts for only about 20 percent of a person's ability to succeed, the rest depends on optimism and learned people skills. A landmark book, *Emotional Intelligence*, by Daniel Goleman, a *New York Times* science writer and Harvard Ph.D., explains why the smartest kid in your high school didn't wind up rich and famous, while the likable kid you barely remember may be a CEO with a happy marriage and a slew of friends: he had a high EQ, which includes the capacity to look on the bright side.

Optimists usually have a high EQ. They recognize that it's not a situation that makes you happy or unhappy, it's your perception of it. Perception is everything! That's why if the morning starts off rocky at home, instead of being irritable the rest of the day, an optimist puts an end to it by deciding to let it go. She then chooses a positive mind-set about whatever will happen next. Happiness for an optimist is always a choice. So even if you're not an intellectual genius—and most of us aren't!—if you'll try to develop positivism, your life is going to improve. It's called *learned optimism*.

One must marry one's feelings to one's beliefs and ideas. That is probably the only way to achieve a measure of harmony in one's life.
—ETTY HILSUM

Talking to Yourself

If you weren't born an optimist who talks positively to yourself, it's time to change. It's a matter of getting out of your rut. Each of us has a concept of our comfort zone, aka rut, in which we function daily. Our insecurity keeps us stuck in our rut. Old verbal habits may be hard to break because you've become so comfortable and stuck with them. Each time you recognize a pessimistic thought, consider it mental malpractice. Flip a switch and think of the positive version. Good habits are formed the same way bad habits are—with practice. It's like learning to talk all over again. Choose words to bolster and support you. That creates a positive feedback loop in your brain. The second you notice yourself talking down, choose to talk on the bright side instead. You deserve better.

Just as when you're choosing a new wardrobe, you can pick words that make you feel more self-confident. Wy, Ash, and I have created many silly sayings to encourage one another. If one is facing a challenge, we gather in a huddle and recite loudly in unison, "What's the last four letters of 'American'? *I CAN!*" It's corny as all get-out, but it's still cheery and sure helps us feel supported.

My therapist taught me to practice the benefits of positive self-talk. It was so effective in helping me heal, it's now become a way of living. I'd say to myself, "I know my body is capable of healing." I've learned to expect positive results.

Scientific research bears out my personal experience. A recent study conducted by the Professional Workforce Survey found that more than 50 percent of the people who approached their challenges with an enthusiastic, positive mind-set were far more effective in their jobs than those who looked upon their situation as problematic. These workers were less likely to get frustrated and anxious; they found themselves to be superior performers overall. Seventy-three percent said they were better able to thrive under the pressure of their situation by taking this positive approach.

Dr. Ed Diener, who researches happiness, found that cheerful people tend to make $14,000 more per year than grouches. Happy folks get more job interviews and are more reliable employees. Although money doesn't buy us happiness, I've learned it's a nice down payment. It's helped calm my nerves. It's simply depressing and troublesome not to have enough money for our necessities. I appreciate the opportunities and mobility that come from financial security. But true success isn't stuff. It's finding out how you have the right stuff.

Few things in the world are more powerful than a positive push. A smile. A word of optimism and hope. A "you can do it" when things are tough. —RICHARD M. DEVOS

An Attitude of Gratitude

Practicing gratefulness is a proven way to reinforce a positive outlook. It's retroactive optimism, because it looks back to generate positive feelings. Gratitude shifts your concentration away from what's not working to notice what's going right in your life. As well as setting your thoughts on an optimistic start for each brand-new day, how about closing your night with a good word? No matter what is going on in your life, you can always find something to be grateful for—even if it's only that things aren't worse.

Larry and I enjoy concluding each night with a ritual of stating our favorite thing that happened. It causes a "great fullness" in our hearts. Last night we both were grateful for the same thing. Elijah and Grace had come over to spend the night. At twilight we sat in the freshly mowed grass of our front yard and sang songs they'd learned at camp. Earlier, I'd signed a contract to do a series on the Food Network, but worldly success can't compare to the intimate joy of watching my grandchildren or relaxing with my husband. It's these small but meaningful everyday moments that give shape and meaning to my days. Start looking into the corners of your life with appreciation and don't overlook the minutiae. Remember the gospel song that says, "Count your blessings, name them one by one." Whenever you and I pause to acknowledge and enjoy what we have, our spirits are uplifted. Our immune system gets a boost. People also enjoy being around us more.

Thanksgiving has always been my favorite holiday 'cause it's about gratefulness, family, friends, food, and fun—my favorite things. When I was struggling with hepatitis C, I'd put my coat on over my pajamas and enter our empty church in the middle of a weekday. I'd kneel at the pulpit and beg God for strength to deal with my trials. After my recovery, Wy and Ash put together a gratefulness family reunion at the farm. It was our end-of-a-season-in-hell benediction. "Benediction" means "good word," the utterance of good wishes at the end of a divine ceremony. Knowing how good we have it helps nurture, comfort, and cushion us when we get knocked down. I'm always touched when I see people on the evening news who've lost everything to some disaster, yet are still thankful just to be alive.

Highly Suggestive

Another way to change your negative beliefs and self-talk is through affirmations. Affirmations are positive, proactive, present-tense statements that you make to yourself. Physiologically, they create a positive feedback loop in your brain. Affirmations have shown to be a therapeutic way to bolster your self-image, especially during times of self-doubt. They induce a calm, confident sense that everything is going to be fine and you are not alone.

Affirmations keep you connected to your higher power. They remind you that through the promises of your birthright as a child of God, you deserve to achieve all your goals, and everything is just the way it's supposed to be. Since you can't have fear and peace in the same thought, affirmations ward off confusing and negative messages from outside sources. That's why it's so important to pray *for the answer—not about the problem.* Someone once asked, "Pray for me, I'm getting the flu." I alerted this person that was a negative prediction. Instead, I suggested we'd pray proactively: *"My body is strong and able to overcome any problem."* Your body is listening and believes and manifests everything you say.

Affirmations also stimulate your subconscious mind as a practical way to speak the truth about your future in advance. They're like going to a mental gym: in order to stay in peak condition, you have to exercise and firm up positive self-beliefs. If I go a few days without making my positive personal affirmations, I don't feel as sharp or strong, and my self-confidence gets flabby and out of shape. Once I get back into my routine and use this technique to get pumped up, I quickly begin to feel better about myself and get back on track.

There are several ways to create your affirmations. Think about your best quality. OK, now what needs reinforcing? Make clear, precise, present-tense statements about whatever you're visualizing for yourself. The statements should be definite and reflect your vision exactly as you see it. Keep them short and powerful.

While getting ready for an appearance, I mentally prepare myself by using an immediate affirmation that puts me in the desired state of mind: "I am a convincing public speaker." A lot of people in the public spotlight—politicians, public speakers, and top business leaders—do this. After carefully preparing for any event, my last step is a quick pep talk. It's a mental version of warming up before working out.

For example, I was recently getting ready to speak onstage at the Houston Astrodome in front of seventy-two thousand people. While the lights were down during my introduction, my security cop, David, drove me out to the center stage in a golf cart. This veteran cop, who knew me from the days of performing with Wy and is now chief of police, was palpably nervous for me. Seventy-two thousand people are a lot of folks, plus the event was being shown on TV! Sitting in the cart, I closed my eyes and did one of my meditative prayers and affirmations. A few minutes later, when the lights went up, I bounded up the steps to the stage. David was flabbergasted at my calmness. Back in the dressing room after the show, I taught him this same technique. He sure can use it in his stressful line of work.

Affirmations can be practiced anywhere—in your car, an elevator, the bathroom, or wherever you find yourself when you need an instant boost. Just find a quiet space where you can visualize the ideal outcome you want and go over the steps needed to get there.

I write my affirmations down and tape them in my Day-Timer so I'm constantly seeing them throughout my day. I'll read them over whenever I'm feeling a little weak in the self-confidence department. You can also record them and then pop them in the tape player in your car. I use the lyrics to Jiminy Cricket's "Whistle a Happy Tune" as an affirmation.

Your Turn Now

What kind of self-talk is going on in your head right now? Eleanor Roosevelt said it best: "No one can make you feel inferior without your permission." If you've been allowing your own mind to berate you, please permit me to point out the switch to turn this off. It's called awareness. Once we become aware of what we are doing and why, we become free to change.

Start talking positively about yourself and your life and notice how things change for the better. Think about reframing as you wake up tomorrow morning. Did you know your first ten minutes of seeing your spouse and kids sets the tone for the entire day?

To gauge your optimism, try completing the following statements. Once you've completed each sentence, read it out loud. Hear yourself make each statement. Do you like what you hear? Would you change any answer if you had the power?

I am good at _____.
I'm known for my _____.
I like my _____.
When I look in the mirror, I see _____.
I always tell myself that I _____.
Today is going to be _____.

I feel good about my _____.
My life is filled with _____.
I've already survived _____.
I know I can achieve _____.

Now try this powerful affirmation:

From this moment, I open up to allow love and healing wisdom to flow through me. My sleep is so deep and restful and my dreams produce solutions and new ideas. I see the good in all things; therefore things evolve to my benefit. People believe in me and trust me to have answers. I have an extremely creative imagination and my intuition serves me well. Whenever I pray, I release my worries and relax even more deeply. I know that God's purposeful good takes over. The higher energy helps me transcend and conquer. I acknowledge my kindness and generosity, and as I do for others, God provides riches that pour into my life. Through this, everything I do blesses and helps other people. I'm a child of the Most High God, which means my birthright is that I'm meant to succeed and be filled with joy.

I release my doubt and fear, and replace them with gratitude in recognition of the gifts that God has bestowed upon me. I'm peaceful, calm, and enjoy living in the moment. I feel peace with everybody and everything. Deep, deep inner strength from God keeps on reminding me what is meaningful in this world. I have all I need. I have people I can trust and depend on, who likewise appreciate my trustworthiness and dependability. I embrace my uniqueness.

It is an indisputable fact that the mind and body are inextricably linked and their second-by-second interaction exerts a profound influence upon health and illness, life and death. Attitudes, beliefs, and emotional states ranging from love and compassion to fear and anger can trigger chain reactions that affect blood chemistry, heart rate, and the activity of every cell and organ system in the body—from the stomach and gastrointestinal tract to the immune system.

—KEN PELLETIER, PH.D., STANFORD CENTER
FOR RESEARCH IN DISEASE PREVENTION

14 Your Mind Is in Every Cell of Your Body

After the initial shock and despair of being diagnosed with hepatitis C, I committed myself to learning everything I could toward saving my life. During meetings with experts in the mind-body connection, I had my next breakthrough understanding, Choice #14: YOUR MIND IS IN EVERY CELL OF YOUR BODY. What that means is that what goes on in your head affects not only your success and peace of mind (as discussed in Chapter 13) but your health as well. That's because there is far less separation between mind and body than we ever thought. I was onto something big!

Here's a summary of what I learned. The brain is a three-pound organ that is a drugstore of hormones and potent neuro-chemicals. Your mind, however, is an information pathway. It's neither physical nor observable. Think of the mind as our body's control tower. Every time we have a thought or experience some feeling, our mind tells our brain to release chemicals that then flow through our body. This cascade of molecules of emotions flows through the bloodstream, then binds at receptor sites on our organs. That's why positive thoughts and happy emotions can actually boost our immune system's functions, while negative thoughts can diminish it. One of the most amazing findings I discovered was that unresolved events or issues from our past have been encoded on a cellular level throughout our body. Now you see why it's so critical to identify and release negative, toxic memories! When you don't pay attention to and then deal with unpleasant emotions and experiences, your body is left to absorb and take over expressing them. The word "symptom" is close to the word "symbol."

As soon as I uncovered this important information, I figured that if my body was listening to everything I was thinking and saying, I'd better begin "medicating" it with positive, life-affirming thoughts! So although doctors somberly warned me to go home to bed, I didn't. Armed with these tantalizing new revelations on how my mind could influence my heath, I risked my life to do a Farewell Concert Tour with Wynonna. Among other benefits, the traveling across all fifty states provided the time and encounters to work through the loss of my beloved stage career. I couldn't afford to permit unresolved grief to harm my already weakened immune system.

The body tends to move along the path of its expectation.

—NORMAN COUSINS

Does the Name "Pavlov" Ring a Bell?

Once I was diagnosed, one of my goals was to understand psychoneuroimmunology. The medical science called psychoneuroimmunology, or PNI, was born in the 1990s. The term was coined by the psychologist Robert Adler. This field of medical science is devoted to understanding the link between the activities of the mind-brain on the immune system. ("Psycho" refers to the brain and mind; "neuro" to the nervous system; and "immunology" to the body's immune system.) The first groundbreaking experiment proving a thought could create a physical response was done by Russian psychologist Ivan Pavlov. Whenever he gave a dog food, Dr. Pavlov rang a bell. With conditioning the dog would eventually salivate at the sound of the bell, even if there was no food. It works on humans too—if you smell a favorite aroma or see an ad for something delicious, you salivate. Next came psychologist Walter Cannon, who showed how fear and danger can produce a panoply of physical reactions that mobilize adrenaline and other hormones to prepare for us a fight. This is called the *fight-or-flight response.*

The fight-or-flight response is useful for a real and present danger—such as a man with a gun pointed at us. We get physically mobilized to fight or run. Our hearts beat faster, the blood vessels in our extremities constrict to prepare our large muscles for combat. But most of us don't fight off armed gunmen all day. The stresses you and I experience are lower-grade but chronic:

waiting in traffic, coping with crying children, dealing with computer crashes. Many of us live with our fight-or-flight reaction on all the time. While stressing our minds, it causes great wear and tear on our bodies. Immune system function goes down when the fight-or-flight system kicks in and stays turned on. It's meant to give us a temporary boost, not be on all the time. What this means is that the more we feel we are in danger, setting off the fight-or-flight response, the more danger we put ourselves in as we strain our immune system and heart.

The power of the imagination is a great factor in medicine. It may produce disease in man and in animals and it may cure them. . . . Ills of the body may be cured by physical remedies or by the power of the spirit acting through the soul. —PARACELSUS

The Feeling-Body Connection

While visiting Ashley in L.A. during the filming of her movie *Heat,* I made an appointment at UCLA's PNI clinic to meet Dr. Margaret Kemeny, Ph.D. Dr. Kemeny is an assistant professor in the department of psychiatry and biobehavioral health at the UCLA School of Medicine, another expert on my list from the *Healing and the Mind* PBS series. I wanted to learn firsthand her research into how emotions can help or hurt the immune system.

As soon as I introduced Ashley, Dr. Kemeny launched into an account of her research involving actors. In her laboratory, actors acted out negative states, such as anger, shock, and sadness, and positive states—joy, love, gratitude. The effects of these emotions on the actors' bodily functions were measured.

The results of either a happy or a sad state were fairly short in duration—twenty to thirty minutes. In varied situations, states of sadness and happiness had different effects on certain immune processes. But it was interesting that both states produced some increase in the activity of natural killer (NK) cells, which help the body fight infection, cancer, and the like. The positive effects of laughter, trust, cuddling, and expressing good feelings improved immune functions.

Dr. Kemeny interpreted this to show that even when actors are displaying a scripted emotion, their bodies still register it. The implications for you? Your body believes you even when you are acting. So fake it to make it.

Another pioneering behavioral medical specialist is James Pennebaker, who also studies how our bodies believe whatever we tell them. Dr. Pennebaker found that being truthful and confessional leads to positive changes within our immune system and overall health. Repressing our thoughts, feelings, and images takes a lot of work. This puts pressure and strain on our autonomic nerve system as well as on our immune system. Choosing to be positive, open, and truthful with our feelings, on the other hand, allows our bodies to operate without that strain. A liar's nose doesn't really grow—but his immune system sure suffers.

For more than two thousand years now, students of Chinese medicine have observed how certain emotions affect specific organs. I studied this ancient form of medicine, which equates parts of the body with essential elements. The heart is equated with the element of fire. Songs and poetry tell us that the heart is identified with happy emotions, such as joy, passion, and love. Scientific research shows that children who have cold and distant parents (often called "refrigerator mothers") are more likely to have heart trouble later in life. Lungs (Wy has asthma) and the large intestine are related to the element of metal, and problems with these have to do with not expressing grief, sadness, worry, and anxiety. Spleen, liver, and stomach, which are associated with the earth, are related to nurturance as well as extensive worrying and thinking too much. Lower back problems, the number-one cause of workmen's disability, are related to a person's emotional center involving money and a fear of lack of support. All this is helpful in identifying our weaknesses so that we can choose healthier responses.

I attended a lecture by Louise Hay about the meaning behind our physical symptoms. For example, she believes that Parkinson's disease may be associated with fear and an overwhelming desire to control. Independent studies support her hypothesis. Doctors report that Parkinson's disease patients have long-term patterns of believing their obligation in life is to uphold standards of morality and champion them. When you don't express your emotions, they will come out sideways!

Because of my liver disease, I was particularly interested in how it, as well as the gallbladder, is equated with wood and tied into emotions of pent-up frustrations and anger, and with having to respond to problems by "smoothing things over." The liver is the most overworked and misunderstood organ. It does a multiplicity of critical functions. The overworked part symbolizes how I felt on tour with the Judds. I was frustrated at having to constantly calm and smooth things over between Wy and myself.

On the positive side, I also learned that the liver is the most regenerative organ in the body. That really resonated for me because my life's theme is all about regeneration!

The scientist who taught me—and the world—that your mind is in every cell of your body is Dr. Candace Pert. She's a neuropharmacologist and research professor in the department of physiology and biophysics at Georgetown University Medical Center. Her groundbreaking work in the 1980s proved not only that our physical organs contain receptor sites for neurochemicals of thought and emotion, but also that our organs and immune systems can manufacture the exact same chemicals. Think about this for a minute! When our brain releases chemicals, the entire body feels and expresses whatever is being felt. All the parts of you are constantly thinking and feeling. Every time you have an emotion, a biochemical molecule called a neuropeptide is made. Dr. Solomon Snyder, a brilliant neuroscientist at Johns Hopkins, further explained to me how our limbic system (the seat of emotions) has an unusually large number of receptor sites for these neuropeptides.

Candace taught me, "You can't separate your brain from your body. Consciousness is not just in the head, nor is it really the question of mind over body. If one takes into account the DNA directing the dance of the peptides, the body is the outward manifestation of the mind."

When I met with her, I learned that because these neuropeptide brain chemicals flow through your body and bind at receptor sites all over your organs, statements like "He makes my skin crawl," "She's a pain in the neck," "I have a gut feeling," "This makes my blood boil," "It makes my heart ache," and "That took my breath away" really are the physical results of your thoughts. For instance, if I called you up onstage to sing with me, you might blush. Your emotion of embarrassment would create an instantaneous physical reaction of facial blood vessels dilating. If you step off a curb and narrowly miss being hit by a car, the scare creates an extreme physical sensation even though nothing has actually happened. Your close call still manifests itself in all sorts of physical ways.

Anytime you repress negative emotions like anger and blame, these thoughts become toxins that get distributed throughout your entire system. While any unexpressed negative feeling can be dangerous physically and emotionally, in this culture the one we handle least well is anger. Anytime you're holding anger in, it's tantamount to being emotionally constipated. The longer you retain it, the more toxic crap keeps getting absorbed in your gut. Conversely, if you explode all the time, you are flooding your body with all kinds of stress hormones. The havoc you wreak on others and yourself creates a ripple effect of unhealthy emotions. That's one of the many reasons why, for your physical, mental, and emotional health and happiness, it's so important to learn to express anger appropriately.

It doesn't take a lot of strength to hang on.
It takes a lot of strength to let go.
—Former U.S. representative J. C. Watts
(who didn't know I'd use his words in this context)

"Anger" Is One Letter Short of "Danger"

Anger is a necessary primal force to help us deal with danger. It comes about whenever you feel you're being trespassed upon or threatened by something or someone. It intensifies unless released.

Anger certainly has its rightful place—for instance, when you react to mistreatment and gross injustices. Anger can be used as a positive source of energy for constructive change. I got so angry at doctors telling me I was doomed by my hepatitis C that I channeled that energy into working on proving them wrong! I got rid of both my anger and my hepatitis C.

But there can be danger in anger too. Do you ever say, "I was so angry I couldn't think straight"? Or "I thought I was going to explode with anger"? Be aware that there can sometimes be a short circuit in the brain that allows anger to drive an action before your intelligence can appropriately intervene. Remember that emotions will drive behavior unless you choose to step back a second and think. The power to choose can make a difference in your health. Anger research shows that the more we let anger run away with us, the more we flood our bodies with stress hormones. When it comes to anger, handling it is all about balance—recognizing that you are angry and not pushing the feeling away, but not lashing out without thinking first. Neuroscientists say that when you are angry, you can develop the ability to step back a second, recognize that you've become angry, and then choose how you want to respond. This state of awareness has even been given a label: meta-mood. Now that you know this, when you are angry you can have a breakthrough (or a breakdown). It's your choice.

I had a breakthrough. I didn't get stuck in toxic anger at the medical establishment, nor did I squander my energy blaming them. To blame is to *b-lame*. To place blame is futile because it never addresses underlying patterns. The best way to stop playing the blame game is simply to refuse to play any longer. Instead, I'm moving forward by working on healing the health care system from within. You too can choose to let anger make you mentally miserable and physically sick, or help you do something constructive and heal.

Research shows that hostility and anger are the number-one predictors for America's biggest killer, heart disease. Anger and hostility are more dangerous than all the risk factors, including smoking and obesity. By the way, I learned an interesting statistic when I worked in cardiac: more heart attacks occur at 9 A.M. on Monday mornings than at any other time.

Anyone can become angry—that's easy. But to be angry with the right person, to the right degree, at the right time, for the right purpose and in the right way—that is not easy. —ARISTOTLE

Don't Let Your Tongue Slash Your Throat

When you angrily confront someone, do you lash out? This only prompts other people to instantly take a defensive stand. They get their hackles up and dig in their heels. Since the best defense is a good offense, they immediately begin coming up with ways to refute whatever you're saying. They're certainly not listening to you! They're busy either preparing to strike back at you or shouting on top of you. It's unlikely either of you will get through to the other one, let alone remember what was said. But you're smarter now, so you have the upper hand. Don't try to match wits with an unarmed person. It certainly may be appropriate to display your anger, but in a controlled and constructive way.

One way I've learned to effectively communicate anger is to replace "you" with "I." This allows you to own your feelings from a personal standpoint. The other person sees how a situation is affecting you. So instead of "You make me so mad," choose "I'm mad." Instead of "You're driving me crazy," try "I'm feeling confused and irritated." Or instead of "You make me look like a fool," say, "I feel upset that I allow you to have power over how I feel about myself."

Your changing the pronoun from "you" to "I" helps the listener better receive your feelings, because it's less of an attack and it gets you closer to a resolution. I call it "pronoun therapy." Confronting others from this more reasonable orientation should incite them to become more civil in response. They'll look down-right foolish if you're mature and controlled.

In addition, avoid using words like "always" and "never"—they make it harder for the other person to agree or change. Interrupting, lecturing, or explaining the other person's behavior is also a definite argument loser. Don't forget—in any and every situation, you must first own your own feelings and change yourself before trying to change someone else. As Indira Gandhi, the former prime minister of India, once said, "You can't shake hands with a clenched fist." As Choice #2 reminds us, when you change your own mind, you change your world. And that will have a ripple effect on others.

Don't find fault, find a remedy. —HENRY FORD

Dear *$!#%+!&

I have personally found that letter writing is a valuable technique for letting go of pent-up anger and sorting out what you might want to say to the person you're mad at. You can decide later whether you should send the letter or not. Sometimes it's appropriate; other times it should remain only with you. So don't decide to send it in the heat of the moment—calm down before you make that decision!

If you need to release anger toward someone who is deceased, writing a letter can be quite cathartic. Louie Anderson, the self-deprecating comedian, was suffering because his abusive alcoholic father had hurt him so deeply. Louie finally wrote a detailed letter to his dad describing the pain he had endured in childhood. He ceremoniously placed it on his dad's grave in Minnesota. Louie said he had experienced a tremendous feeling of relief from the act and gained a sense of closure from the process.

Letter writing allows you the advantage of taking all the time you need to get in touch with whatever got you upset. It permits you to express your anger as clearly and strongly as you need. You have the option of going back and rewriting until you're completely satisfied. A letter also allows the reader to be alone when reading it. Your words can actually enter the offender's mind. He or she can refer back to the letter if unclear about any of your statements. By the way, I always make and keep a copy of my letters before I send them.

When I received a letter of apology from an ex-employee Wy and I had sent to alcohol rehab, I learned that one of the twelve steps of Alcoholics Anonymous requires people in recovery to make amends to someone they've hurt. Therapy by letter writing has been around a long time.

The written word may be man's greatest invention. It allows us to converse with the dead, the absent, and the unborn.
—ABRAHAM LINCOLN

Judd Family Feud Rules

No one can push our buttons better than our own family! They know all our stuff, so we are most vulnerable to them. F. Scott Fitzgerald thought so. He said, "Family quarrels are bitter things. They don't go according to any rules. They're not like aches or wounds; they're more like splits in the skin that won't heal because there's not enough material."

It's taken many years of hurt feelings, tantrums, and unre-solved conflicts for my family to get to where we are now! I'd say our family now represents "enlightened imperfection." The room for improvement will always be the biggest room at the Judd house. Everyone got together at the kitchen table one night after supper and came up with guidelines for communicating difficult things. Here's what we've all agreed on:

1   No interrupting. (Wy used to say I'd make a great parole officer because I never let her finish her sentences.)

2   No shouting.

3   Everyone must realize we each have our own reality. (This is a big one for all family members to grasp.)

4   Everyone gets as much time as they need to fully express themselves.

5   Everyone should be prepared with their thoughts and solutions so time isn't wasted. This encourages the quiet, introverted ones to participate.

6   Pause to think before you speak so you address the person as a friend.

7   No fair bringing others' opinions into it. (Example: "So-and-so said . . .")

8   Silence can be another form of arguing. Say what's on your mind.

9   Everyone needs to be aware that there will always be some "issue."

Our commitment to communicating is the bottom line to making sure our family endures. The door is always open here at the Judd house. Our hearts are never closed.

Learning and following these rules can help you keep your family strong and together. Remember, if you demand, "My way or the highway," you may risk not seeing a family member or friend again. Conflict can't survive without your participation. Confrontation gets easier when you choose to give up your need to be right. No matter how you slice it, there are always two sides. When in doubt, ask yourself: would you rather be happy or right?

Better to pick a lock than kick the door down.

—HENRY, BELLMAN AT THE PEABODY HOTEL, MEMPHIS, TENNESSEE

Your Turn Now

Are you prolonging anger and hiding behind it like a dark veil? Has your anger become a wall of smugness separating you from a chance to be whole? "Mad" spelled backwards is "dam," which as you know walls off and holds back a natural current. Releasing anger will eventually lead to compassion for others. Like an emotional vasodilator, it can even open a heart that has been constricted!

Just don't lose it. Refer to the Judd Family Feud Rules to create your own United Nations treaty, and consult the tips below. Think clearly before acting. If you or someone you know has uncontrolled bouts of anger, please check out anger management resources such as therapy or books. Good books include *The Dance of Anger,* by Harriet Lerner, and *Getting over Getting Mad,* by Judy Ford.

Some tips for controlling anger:

- Don't let someone else's bad manners ruin your good manners. If you do, they win.

- Redirect your anger by spotting the cause and observing as a bystander. Any extreme reaction to whatever has upset you has a lot of energy around it. An angry outburst has valuable information in it that you can use to learn more about yourself. Use it.

- Find a way to distract yourself until you calm down.

- Make yourself be quiet and simply listen to the person with whom you disagree.

- Laugh at yourself and the stupidity of it all.

- Remember the Golden Rule: "Do unto others as you would have them do unto you."

- Don't get personal with your adversary; instead, take the team approach by asking, "How can we find a solution here?" Base all your words on solving the problem. It will neutralize the other's personal sense of affront and also get you moving forward.

- Your goal in an argument should be not to win but to make progress.

As I was walking up the stair
I met a man who wasn't there.
He wasn't there again today.
I wish, I wish he'd stay away.

—HUGHES MEARNS

15 Worry and Fear Are Dispensable Parasites on Your Brain

I feared something was really wrong. I had felt crummy off and on for two years. The periods of flulike symptoms were becoming more intense and lasting longer. Then came that moment in the doctor's office when he proclaimed that I had hepatitis. In that earliest diagnosis, back in 1990, it was simply called "non-A, non-B." Later hepatitis C was identified and I was diagnosed with it. Along with the hepatitis virus came side effects—worry and fear.

Fear is pain about the future. The panic-producing prognosis of less than three years to live meant I had no future. What time I had would be miserable. Because I understood Choice #14—*Your mind is in every cell of your body*—I knew I had to confront, then learn how to control my fear. I couldn't allow myself to indulge in anxiety, because I knew my body would turn the doctor's prognosis into a self-fulfilling prophecy.

I was also constantly worried. Worry is pain about the present. Worry is like sitting in a rocking chair. It gives you something to do, but doesn't get you anywhere. Worry and fear occupy different temporal locations in our brains. Worry is more of a generalized, free-floating anxiety. It's the most common form of mental activity. Of the ten thousand thoughts you and I have in a single day, believe it or not, five thousand of them are worries. When we are worried, we need to check out whether our anxiety is based on something real or our imagination is running away with us.

With my diagnosis came a number of dramatic, present-tense worries—including waiting for a biopsy report and lab results, canceling concert dates, breaking the news to my family and friends, band and crew, reassuring Ash it was okay to move to Hollywood, and coming up with a plan to help Wynonna to prepare for a solo career.

I couldn't allow worry and fear to cloud my thinking while making these serious decisions. Negative emotions would prey on my immune system. By now I knew my brain was a drugstore, so in addition to the interferon I was taking, I needed to prescribe the healing bromides of optimism and hope for my immune system. I had to learn Choice #15: WORRY AND FEAR ARE DISPENSABLE PARASITES ON YOUR BRAIN.

Fortunately, one of my experts in the mind-body field explained to me that you can't have two contradictory thoughts at the same instant. When something is worrying you, you can pause, then choose to replace the worry by coming up with a specific action that negates or solves the issue. I made a list of my worries and, with the help of my therapist, came up with steps I could take toward solving each dilemma. For example, my hand would be shaking when my doctor phoned with lab results. Instead of giving him authority (like the Wizard of Oz), I paused to remember it was My Body. I prayed for healing as I listened, and envisioned my virus being devoured by an army of white cells. Taking positive action helped—my worries began to diminish!

Being in charge of your emotions like this gives you a sense of control and mastery. Once I discovered the power of taking action to replace worry, I began to use it all the time. For instance, because I travel so much and stay in hotels, sometimes I worry I could be in a fire. But I take action by staying on the second or third floors, so if I had to, I could jump. I check out the nearest emergency exit and fire instructions. I even started carrying a smoke mask in my overnight satchel. Then I release the worry!

Whatever challenges you and I are facing, it is imperative that we choose to change our mind and become proactive in addressing our worries. We simply can't afford the high price our bodies pay for the stress of worry.

These days, if I find that I'm holding on to some worry, I choose to be proactive. I do a breathing exercise, slowly inhaling through my nose. I breathe in calmness and serenity. Then I identify the worry and exhale it noisily through my mouth. It really helps! It's free and you can do it anywhere, anytime.

Another trick I've learned to stop worrying is mood words. Because your mind can't hold two contradictory thoughts at once, I say out loud positive, calming words that switch my mind from worry to tranquillity. I wind up feeling not only more relaxed and at peace, but also more in charge. Try words like these: SLOW DOWN . . . BREATHE . . . PEACE . . . ABUNDANCE . . . LOVING-KINDNESS . . . UNIFY . . . GRATEFULNESS . . . GLORIFY . . . SERENITY . . . MAGNIFICENCE . . . BLISS.

I also summon my guardian angels. As a child playing on my grandparents' farm, I had an imaginary friend I considered my guardian angel. Her name was Elizabeth. Now I realize I have many. I've even written a children's book called *Guardian Angels,* illustrated with the likenesses of the farm and my grandmother, to help children realize their angels are always with them. When I find myself caught up in some worry, I envision these divine, protective, angelic archetypes standing guard all around me. So far, I've found over three hundred scriptures in the Bible pertaining to guardian angels. They are a real spiritual resource, but you and I must use free will to summon them into action.

If your worry involves a phobia, as of heights or flying, expose yourself to the fear by taking a short plane ride with an understanding companion who makes you feel comfortable. Doing this behavior over and over until the phobia is gone is called *exposure therapy*.

Worry never gets you anywhere. A quiet, calm mind clears the way for clarity and constructive planning. Doing all you can by planning, calm breathing, using specific mood words, calling on angels, and remembering to be in God's presence are all proactive moves that help you live contentedly in the moment. Be sure to reward yourself when you do master your worry. It will give you incentive to keep on stamping out the worry bug.

Tell yourself that everything you visualize is already there. Everything is energy. Everything vibrates at its own level of reality. Having a thought about what you'd like to see happen for yourself, it is nothing more than connecting the two frequencies together to make the reality happen for you. —WAYNE DYER

False Evidence Appearing Real

From the morning paper to the evening news, our society makes us anxious: terrorist attacks, ATM shootings, suicide bombers, anthrax, unsafe meat, shark attacks, child molesters, road rage, to name just a few. The abiding rule for priority placement of a news story in any newsroom is "If it bleeds, it leads." Every day the news breaks into our home, preying on our fears, robbing us of our power, and rendering us ineffective. Have you ever come in from a good day, turned on the news, and felt your mood darkening? TV allows fear into your home, which should be your sanctuary.

Fear is the darkroom where our negatives develop. The acronym FEAR stands for *false evidence appearing real.* If you don't identify and release your fear, it will leave you powerless and unable to stand up for yourself. An unresolved fear can also develop into an illness and then go on to prevent you from recuperating. Fear is the greatest inhibitor of the human spirit. Fear thrives on a lack of self-confidence and prevents us from taking risks. Since risk enables us to become what we're meant to be, we can't allow our fears to paralyze us into mediocrity. Humans are born with only two fears—of loud noises and of falling. The rest are learned and therefore can be unlearned.

Most of us think that we shouldn't act if we feel fear. But the trick to eliminating the parasite of fear is—to quote the title of the Susan Jeffers book on the subject—*Feel the Fear and Do It Anyway.* Rather than waiting till they're not afraid, people who want to make something of their lives acknowledge their fear and do what they want in spite of it. Then the fear is diminished because they have had the experience of success. Once on *The Tonight Show,* Jay Leno asked Wynonna what her biggest fear was. "I can sum it up in five words," she said. " 'Live TV with my mom.' " But there she was—on live TV, sitting beside me. Like Wy, in order for us to blossom to our fullness, we must choose to be proactive, despite our fear. Nothing scares me anymore. I've raised Wy and Ash.

Our fears are more numerous than our dangers, and we suffer more in our imagination than in reality. —SENECA

Meditation Means "Good Medicine"

One very effective way to eliminate worry and fear over the long term is to meditate. Meditation creates a sense of self-mastery, inner stillness, and stability. This newfound calmness supplants worry and fear. There's even new research showing that meditation actually changes your mind's inclination to feel negative emotions like fear and worry, replacing it with the tendency to feel positive emotions like hope, optimism, and gratitude. I'm now hooked on it.

Meditation also strengthens your inner witness, the deeper part of yourself that becomes more and more aware of the movement of your thoughts. With a strong inner witness, you are aware of your worries and fears without getting overly involved with them. "Oh, there I go, getting afraid about money again." "Oops, there I am worrying about my daughter." You begin to notice that while such thoughts do arise, they also disappear, all on their own.

When I first began to meditate, I'd picture my mind like the ocean. It may start out with huge, pounding waves of scary thoughts and feelings. I allow it to wash over me, and eventually the surface does calm down. It becomes tranquil and serene. Each time a wave starts to kick up, I gently bring my attention to it and focus on allowing it to abate literally and metaphorically. The waters must be perfectly calm to reflect the heavens.

Jon Kabat-Zinn and his staff at the University of Massachusetts Memorial Medical Center have been teaching meditation to patients battling chronic pain, anxiety, and depression. You can read more on how to learn the practice of meditation in his book *Full Catastrophe Living*.

The following is Jon's meditation suggestion for beginners. You may want to begin with five or ten minutes and increase the time gradually. Some people like to record these instructions and listen to them as they meditate. You may want to use a timer so you won't need to keep checking your watch.

Sit comfortably in a chair with your head, neck, and back straight but not stiff. Make sure your shoulders are relaxed. Place your hands comfortably in your lap or on your knees. Allow your feet to rest flat on the floor. Loosen any clothing that's too tight. Allow your eyes slowly to close.

Feel your belly gently expand and recede, rising with each in-breath and falling with each out-breath. With each out-breath, feel your body become more relaxed. Become aware of your feet resting on the floor, or your legs and buttocks against the chair, or your back against the back of the chair. Now become aware of your breath as it passes by the nostrils, back and forth, in and out.

When thoughts arise, notice them. Then let them go. If sensations appear in your body, notice them. Then let them go. Bring your attention back to your breathing each time it wanders off, and simply experience each in-breath as it comes into your body and each out-breath as it leaves

*your body. Feel or imagine the breath moving through your
body: down into your chest, your belly, your legs, and
your toes on each in-breath, and up from your toes, legs,
belly, and chest on each out-breath.*

*As best you can, avoid judging yourself or your
thoughts or feelings. Just note them, trying not to pursue
them or reject them. You see clearly what is here in this
moment, and then let it be. Return to the breath,
maintaining moment-to-moment awareness as it
continues to move in and out of your body.*

*At the end of the time, allow your eyes to open, and
gradually accustom yourself to the world around you. You
may well find that the feelings of relaxation, awareness,
and acceptance that you have just experienced will deepen
as you continue to meditate.*

Don't Panic

Sometimes fear and worry get out of control and you need professional help. Unfortunately, I know this firsthand. Even though
it happened a while ago, as I start to tell this story about one of the
worst things that ever happened to me, my heart begins to beat a
little quicker.

I was on the bus with Wynonna and my mom, headed for
our first show after I had gotten so sick with hepatitis C. Even
though I was in the most familiar place imaginable, "my womb"
(as I called my room on our bus, the Dream Chaser), I awakened
at three in the morning hallucinating. I thought I was going
crazy. I wondered if I was dying. An unexplainable vicious cycle
of thoughts began. I seemed to be floating in a bubble. My once
familiar surroundings were strange and surreal. My heart was
racing and I was sweating (I rarely sweat). A pressure headache

made me feel as if I were wearing a tight skullcap. Hyperventilating caused me to become even shorter of breath.

As I got out of bed, my legs were weak and shaky. I felt nauseous and my vision was blurry. The tightness in my chest, the numbness and tingling in my fingertips made me question if I was having a heart attack. I felt intensely afraid and sensed I was in imminent mortal danger. I tore open the bus window curtains to see that we were driving in a blinding snowstorm. This contributed to an increasing claustrophobic sense of being smothered. I quickly took off my pajama top and pressed my bare breasts against the frosted window in an attempt to shock myself into reality. Hello, passing truckers!

The attack gradually subsided over the next three hours, leaving me shaky and disturbed. When we arrived at our hotel, my sister-in-law, Middy Judd, who is a nurse, was waiting there with my brother, Mark. Middy hugged me after I described my symptoms and gently explained, "Oh honey, you're having a panic attack."

Just hearing that there was a definite diagnosis made me breathe a slight sigh of relief. When we know what's wrong, we can start to figure out how to make it better. I was already aware of the fight-or-flight syndrome, which is necessary for us to avoid real danger. But with panic attacks, sometimes the nervous system delegating this response gets disrupted and a person feels threatened by totally innocuous situations.

I went straight to my therapist as soon as we got home. She explained that a panic attack is an irrational act of the mind. But since the mind is like a control tower, routing messages throughout your body, your symptoms are very real. Panic attacks are an explicit example of how your mind affects your body. Thoughts create changes in neurotransmitters and hormones, which precipitate physical symptoms. Then, of course, it becomes a feedback loop as these physical symptoms go back and create changes in neurotransmitters and hormones. The cycle begins again.

About three-fourths of *panic attack disorder* patients are women between twenty and thirty-five years old. It's very uncommon for such an attack to occur for the first time in the elderly. The cyclically changing hormonal levels of a woman's reproductive years may be responsible in part for the onset of panic attacks. This was true for me.

I cannot overstate the fact that panic attacks are not the result of a character flaw or emotional weakness. Famous friends who've suffered from debilitating panic attacks include Carly Simon and Donny Osmond. At one point Oscar-winning actress Kim Basinger couldn't even leave her house for a long period of time. When I testified on Capitol Hill, in Washington, D.C., our panel of experts stressed that panic disorders affect emotionally healthy people. Approximately 22.7 million Americans, 12 percent of our population, will suffer from panic attacks or other anxiety disorders at some point in their lives. They are very real and they're serious. The good news is that they are treatable with therapy and medication. So it's tragic that only one-third of the people suffering a panic attack get any treatment. Spread the word: there's help and hope!

I'm now cured of panic attacks, but if you or someone you know is suffering from them, be sure to get professional help. I highly recommend a book called *Triumph over Fear*, by Jerilyn Ross.

There are hazards in anything one does, but there are greater hazards in doing nothing. —SHIRLEY WILLIAMS

The Depression Demon

When I appeared on Donny and Marie Osmond's TV talk show, Marie shared with me in private her battle with another mental health problem—postpartum depression. Like panic attacks, it's another form of anxiety that's hormonally driven.

Postpartum depression is just one of the forms of clinical depression. Other types include bipolar disorder, seasonal affective disorder, and major depressive disorder. Clinical depression is more than just feeling blue or down in the dumps for a while. It is a serious condition that affects the ability to work, eat, sleep, or enjoy the normal pleasures of life. People suffering from depression can't "just snap out of it," nor can they will themselves to feel better.

Depression in all its forms is a worldwide health crisis—the World Health Organization estimates that depression is the fourth leading cause of disability in the world. It is the most common psychiatric disorder; women have a 10 to 25 percent chance of suffering from it at least once in their lives, and men between 5 and 12 percent.

According to the National Institute of Mental Health, signs of depression include

- sadness, hopelessness, pessimistic or empty feelings

- trouble concentrating, making decisions, or remembering

- decreased energy, fatigue

- inability to sleep or oversleeping

- loss of interest in activities you once enjoyed, including sex

- significant weight loss or gain

- restlessness, irritability, or excessive crying

- feelings of helplessness, worthlessness, or guilt

- thoughts of death or suicide, or suicide attempts

- aches and pains and other physical symptoms that don't respond to treatment

Very effective treatments for all forms of depression are now available, most usually a combination of drugs and therapy. Unfortunately, experts estimate that only one-third of those suffering from depression seek treatment. If you or someone you love is depressed—please get help as soon as possible! Not wanting to get out of bed, leave the house, or talk to others makes it hard to take the first step. But 80 to 90 percent of depressed folks who receive treatment feel better in only a few weeks. See your family doctor to get a referral to a psychiatrist (a doctor who can prescribe drugs and also does therapy), or visit a community mental health clinic. Your employer may also have employee assistance programs that make referrals.

If you know someone who suffers from postpartum blues, I recommend Marie's book *Behind the Smile*. Good self-help books on general depression include *Undoing Depression*, by Richard O'Connor, and *Breaking the Patterns of Depression*, by Michael Yapko.

For God hath not given us the spirit of fear, but of power and of love and of a sound mind. —II TIMOTHY 1:7

Your Turn Now

When I appeared on *Larry King Live* on a panel about mental disorders such as panic attacks and depression, Larry was surprised that he received the most call-ins the long-running show has ever had. Information is our power in dealing with any illness or crisis. Remember: you have a danger, but you also have an opportunity. The opportunity is for you to take stock of your life and start getting the help you need. These choices will help you transform your life for the better.

If, however, you have just the normal parasites of worry and fear, try the techniques I suggested in this chapter, along with these others:

- When you start to picture something going wrong, remember you're in charge of telling your mind what to think. You can direct and produce all the scenes going on in your brain. You can rehearse the same scene but work out a happy ending to it. Focus on a positive outcome. If you drift to a negative, refocus on good so you can close your eyes and tell yourself, "I'm the director in this story. I can change this right now, this very instant."

- Try the technique I personally use, called "riding the wave." If I feel an incoming wave of anxiety, I imagine myself on top of it like a surfer girl. Then, just as I would have to do if I were in the physical experience, I go with the flow as it crests. I teach myself to control my inhalations and elongate them, and then I slowly purse my lips and breathe out strongly. I remember that it's happened before and I overcame it.

- List the five things you fear most. Examine the origin of each. Figure out one step you can take to overcome them. In your mind's eye, identify each fear and attach it to an imaginary balloon and set it free over your head. Let it float away into the atmosphere until it disappears from sight.

- Make your home a sanctuary, a psychological fortress. Be sure it's comfy, calm, and pleasing so it can be your heart's resting place. Decorate with objects that give you fond memories of who you are. They will help you keep centered and stable.

- Join a support group. Talk to a friend who understands.

- Distract yourself with exercise or a relaxing hobby.

- Read or watch inspiring stories of people who have overcome their problems.

- Practice your faith. I realize that everything happens for a reason, as part of a larger plan to grow in love and wisdom and be of service, so I don't take problems personally. I trust in a divine intelligence smarter than I, which helps me relax in my life. *Fear knocked at the door. Faith answered. No one was there.*

Remember, there are always going to be things to be afraid of and worried about. But you and I get to decide which ones are real threats. Then we can choose how to handle them. Will you join me in choosing peace and happiness from now on?

Aim for success, not perfection. Never give up your right to be wrong, because then you will lose the ability to learn new things and move forward with your life.

—Dr. David M. Burns

---

16 Resign as General Manager of the Universe

*H*ear me out before you want to slug me: illness or other challenges can actually be a blessing as well as a curse. They allow us to take stock of our lives and adapt to new ways. One beneficial thing hepatitis C did for me was to make me face up to some destructive behaviors.

Hepatitis C can flatten you like a pancake. Since the liver stores glycogen (the body's source of energy), with my inflamed liver I didn't have the energy to indulge my usual perfectionistic tendencies. Relegated to bed, I sat watching as my husband folded laundry the wrong way. Horrors! My mother, who'd come to help out, was putting pots and pans in the wrong kitchen cabinet. Egad! Ashley (aka the Human Tornado) was home from college, and her activities were leaving behind a trail throughout the house.

Suddenly, Hurricane Wynonna blew in. Her nickname indicates that, like the weather, you cannot control or predict this force of nature. She proudly announced she'd bought a big surprise to cheer me up. Wy ceremoniously plopped a cute white Westie puppy onto my bed. It immediately peed. As the soaking went through my spread, blankets, sheets, and onto me, I went into a perfectionist spasm. Larry, Mom, Ash, and Wy gathered around on the bed, laughing their butts off while merrily playing with the puppy. At that very moment I had a breakthrough. I decided to do some emotional housecleaning and embrace Choice #16: RESIGN AS GENERAL MANAGER OF THE UNIVERSE. I could no longer be my old perfectionist, do-it-all self. It wasn't an option—I just didn't have the strength. Besides, it was standing in the way of having more fun and pleasure.

Finality is death. Perfection is finality. Nothing is perfect. There are lumps in it. —JAMES STEPHENS

Try On a Pink Slip

The expression "What's wrong with this picture?" originated with a cartoon that you were supposed to study closely in order to spot what was wrong or missing. The catch in this exercise is that the viewer usually doesn't pay attention to what's right about the picture, let alone even notice the overall picture—they're singularly focused on finding fault. This is precisely what happens when you or I are being perfectionistic. We're standing outside of life nitpicking at little things, finding fault, and then judging. Meantime, we're not fully participating in or occupying our lives, let alone enjoying ourselves.

On the set of Ashley's thriller *The Blackout Murders* I met Carol, one of the people on a movie set who get paid to play "What's wrong with this picture?" The continuity person makes sure all details are the same from scene to scene: "No, last time her hair was parted on the left, now it's on the right." Carol admitted how hard it was to turn off this kind of close observation in her real life. But she's not really a perfectionist. She just plays one for the movies.

Kelsey Grammer once had me do a call-in for his popular show, *Frasier,* in which he plays a talk show psychologist. I was to play an uptight perfectionist. Frasier's on-air advice to me was "Next time your perfectionist tendencies hinder you, remember this quotation from Henry James: 'Excellence does not require perfection.'" How true! While it's important to strive for personal excellence, we don't have to be perfect. You and I are already enough. In fact, it is our imperfections that make us unique and real. A Navajo rug weaver in Sedona, Arizona, once told me the Navajo wisdom on this subject as she pointed out a purposeful flaw in her rug: "We believe if we attain perfection, our life is over."

You and I can't pay attention to the picture if we're busy dusting the frame. As I took in the whole picture of my family in that moment when the dog peed on my bed, something in my mind shifted. Instead of narrowly focusing on the imperfections, my eyes opened to how lucky I was to have a close, loving family around me who cared so much. The hum of our household's daily activity, the sound of familiar laughter, and the playful noises of an adorable puppy were the beautiful music and rhythm of my life. I decided to start dancing to it. Care to join me?

The rewards were immediate. It was a relief to not always have to lead. Others were just as capable, and it was time for those who weren't to begin to learn. The girls began to see the bigger picture themselves. They saw me as a vulnerable human being instead of Supermom come to this planet to clean up their messes. Hepatitis C was my kryptonite, and they became protective and attentive to me. Wy, Ash, Larry, and Mom enjoyed feeling needed, and our interdependence drew us even closer. These days I'm a recovering perfectionist and much happier. (So are those who live with me.) Anytime they suspect I'm relapsing, their code phrase is "Mom, go wash a load."

You need to loosen your grip. —DIANE ATKINSON

Do You Have the Dis-ease to Please?

Nowadays, I get a kick out of watching the reactions of women on airplanes as the stewardess instructs, "In an emergency, adjust your own oxygen mask first before attempting to help adjust others'." I can see them resisting, 'cause it's counterintuitive. Yet a mother with small children must first be fully conscious so she can care for them. In every way, the best mom is one who begins by taking care of herself. Mothers who are martyrs set a terrible example. As the popular phrase warns, "If Mama isn't happy, ain't nobody happy." The best dad is one who knows it's more important to please his family than his company. And the best thing a father can do for his kids is love their mother.

If your tendency is to make everyone else a priority, putting everyone else's needs above your own, it means you consider your innate value to be less than theirs. Uh-oh—definite indicator of very low self-esteem. Why in the world are you even for a second holding a belief that other people's needs are somehow more urgent and important than your own? If you don't care about your own problems and needs, who the heck do you think will?

Women's brains are hardwired to multitask. We are natural managers. If you're like me, you sincerely want to help others and take charge. Fine—as long as you first take care to *manage* your own time, *take charge* of your own thoughts, *help* yourself, and *supervise* the way others treat you. People will treat you the way you've trained them to.

Take a look into the Mirror of Truth here: on a scale of one to ten, how much of a people pleaser are you? The surefire cure for being a people pleaser is to stare at yourself in the mirror and ask: "What is my motivation here?" As you penetrate below excuses and rationales, you'll see the answer most likely lies in a poor sense of self-worth. Why on earth would you feel that you're not good enough just being yourself?

What I discovered when I turned in my pink slip on running the world is that you and I have to be willing to disappoint somebody else in order to be true to ourselves. Now I use phrases like "I can't, but I'll show you how." And "No." It's a terrific word! I like it a lot these days. "No" is now my word of choice whenever I'm feeling pressure, obligation, or resentment. I began to realize that I wasn't always doing the other person a favor if I continued to do for them. I was just being an enabler for their weaknesses. Now I tell folks, "I'm my current project" and "Sorry, my plate's already full." Another word I found is "delegate." Rather than do it myself, I began to appoint and oversee competent others.

When we fall for the notion that we need to be in charge of everything, we're not standing up for ourselves. It harms our relationships, self-esteem, and even health because stress from doing too much increases the deleterious hormones cortisol and catecholamine norepinephrine.

We don't see things as they are, we see them as we are. —ANAÏS NIN

Mine and Yours

By acknowledging your needs and saying "No," you set important distinctions between your needs and others' demands. The poet Robert Frost was right: "Good fences make good neighbors." Good emotional boundaries help us understand where we end and others begin. Each of us has an invisible territorial perimeter, usually about three feet. Doesn't it make you uncomfortable when someone, especially a stranger, stands too close? Obviously, if someone shoves us or touches us suggestively, they're trespassing. Emotional boundaries are every bit as necessary to define and protect our individuality and character. Until we decide what ours are, we'll be unclear what we're responsible for and what we aren't.

"Codependent" describes someone who's emotionally reliant on another person who's caught in an addiction like alcohol or gambling. Codependents have such low self-esteem that they feel valued only when they align themselves with someone who will always need them. Think of it as emotional slavery by mutual consent. Misery loves company.

Stop here for a minute and think about your significant other. Are you really clear about where your needs end and his or hers begin? If you don't have boundaries, you may wind up giving yourself away.

I became even more aware of the importance of appropriate physical and emotional boundaries from a masseuse who volunteers her services to newborn blind babies in a hospital nursery. A blind baby doesn't know where it begins and ends. It dawned on me how touch can not only establish physical and emotional boundaries but also disrupt them, as a result of unwanted physical advances. A healthy or unhealthy outcome depends on the other party's intentions.

Too many women don't understand the importance of setting healthy boundaries. In any relationship, it's critical that women have good physical, emotional, and sexual boundaries. Mothers who are people pleasers send bad signals of unworthiness to their kids. Teenage girls aren't taught self-esteem and how to say "No." Instead, they are taught to put the other person's feelings first. And that spells trouble as they begin to date. Small children need to bond and identify with their caregiver as they're growing. But they need to begin disengaging as they reach their teens. By adulthood, they should have a firm sense of where they end and others begin. Unfortunately, in today's culture, rather than learning healthy boundaries, impressionable teens are being influenced by negative role models through the media. Peer pressure from other teens who have also fallen prey to bad influences has an exponentially harmful effect.

No matter your age, you must establish boundaries. As you learn more about what you like and don't like, you can better explain it to others. Establishing emotional boundaries allows you to prevent your self-respect and character from being intruded upon.

Never, for the sake of peace and quiet, deny your own experience or convictions. —DAG HAMMARSKJÖLD

Could That Be a Control Freak in Your Mirror of Truth?

Some people have inappropriate boundaries in the other direction. They intrude on others' boundaries as they try to control other people's behavior and invade their space. People who insist on being dominant and in control think the only way they can maintain their self-respect is by constantly asserting themselves. They constantly break rules, don't carry out instructions, insist on doing things their own way, and buy into the philosophy that it's a jungle, a rat race. But as Lily Tomlin says, even if you win, you're still a rat.

Any need for control is rooted in fear—the fear of not getting what you want or the fear of losing what you have. Neediness results in manipulation: Control or be controlled. But we can't control another person's behavior, no matter how hard we try. We can control our reactions, though. That's enough.

The next time someone disappoints you, stand back and watch whether you resort to control and manipulation. It's such a waste of time and energy. Hasn't it occurred to you that they're on their own path and timeline? Bless 'em as they go.

Not only can you not control other people, you can't control how they're going to perceive you, either. They'll always be projecting their own issues onto you and judging you based on preconceived notions from their own experiences. If all you've been caring about is how other people see you, your life is nothing but a reflection of how somebody else thinks. What a waste!

If you're feeling a general dissatisfaction with how your life's going, it may well be because you've forgotten who the heck you are. Have you been pretending so long you've forgotten you're pretending?

If I am not for myself, who will be for me? If I am not for others, who am I for? And if not now, when? —THE TALMUD

Your Turn Now

Next time you're carefully backing out of a room you've just vacuumed so you don't leave footprints on the perfectly symmetrical impressions in the carpet . . . stop! How about resigning as general manager of the universe? Come join me in dancing to the music of life! Let's boogie:

- Are you a doormat for other people to wipe their feet on?

- Do you have too few boundaries? Do you allow other people to control you?

- Who enters your space (bathroom, bedroom, office)? How and when? Do they ask permission or just barge in?

- Identify two ways you honor yourself with privacy. (For instance, no one bothers me when I am on the phone.)

- How impressionable were you as a teen? What sort of peer pressure were you subjected to? How do you hold your own in a group of peers now?

- Do you ever catch yourself changing the subject, leaving the room, being late, feigning illness, or refusing to pay attention when faced with a situation or an individual who's making you feel uncomfortable? All are possible clues of a fear of confrontation stemming from boundary issues.

- Do you ever defend your refusal to stand up for your position with "It wouldn't do any good anyway," "He doesn't understand," "My case is different," "Nobody else does it," or "I don't want to rock the boat"?

- Do other people force their ideas on you? Do they assume they already know your preferences?

- Do you feel taken for granted? Do others interrupt or talk on top of you? Are your interests unacknowledged or passed over? Do people share inappropriately intimate information with you? (Being submissive is a ploy to earn approval and acceptance.)

- Do you overeat or use alcohol to "nurture" yourself? Do you pass up health checkups because you don't have time for yourself?

The behaviors I just listed are the results of thoughts such as "I can't cope as well as other people," "I'm not good at making decisions on my own," "I need others to tell me what to do," "I shouldn't say anything that will ruffle the feathers or offend," and "If I'm not loved or needed, I have no chance to ever be happy." You can change those thoughts!

When it comes to doing too much and having inappropriate boundaries, I've found that the revised Serenity Prayer helps a lot:

God grant me the serenity to accept the people I cannot change, the courage to change the one I can, and the wisdom to know it's me.

Amen!

The great and glorious masterpiece of humanity is to know how to live with purpose. —MONTAIGNE

17 Find a New, Stronger Life Urge

According to renowned psychologist Carl Jung, our most distressing problems (such as death, illness, and betrayal) are fundamentally unsolvable. What he means is that life isn't fair or easy. OK, I'll buy that. But we do have a choice about what we do with what happens. Jung suggests that whatever calamity we're facing loses its urgency when we make Choice #17: FIND A NEW, STRONGER LIFE URGE. This is revolutionary! It's how we can keep our sanity and move forward.

I began discovering this breakthrough truth while lying on my supposed deathbed. Studying everything I could about hepatitis C, I was horrified to learn that over 4 million Americans currently have the disease and that it will kill four times as many Americans as AIDS in the next decade. When I heard these grim statistics, despite how awful I felt, I had an urge to call the 1-800 number of the American Liver Foundation (ALF) to ask how I could become involved. The ALF had no money or figurehead. Although at the time I couldn't even help myself, much less others, I decided it would become my new goal to raise awareness and money. I volunteered to become its spokesperson. I am convinced that this choice helped me heal.

Over the next couple of days, I noticed that focusing on this greater purpose took my mind off some of my misery. As I projected myself into the future by committing to activities on behalf of the ALF, I was affirming in my mind, body, and spirit that I would indeed outlive this crisis and turn it into something positive.

To replace the omnipresent fear of losing my health, self-esteem, and identity, I chose a new life urge—beating my disease and then using what I learned to help others in my situation. I had already been easing the aftershock of some of my past calamities by speaking out about teen pregnancy and family planning, welfare reform, and battered women. Now I wanted to be a witness for those with hepatitis C. I chose a reason to get out of bed and go on living.

Man's main concern is not to gain pleasure or to avoid pain but rather to see a meaning in his life. That is why man is even ready to suffer, on the condition, to be sure, that his suffering has a meaning. —Viktor Frankl

---

Transforming Our Suffering

Our everyday challenges offer the possibility of coming up with a new purpose for living. Right now, if I have to describe myself, the first two words that immediately pop out are "optimistic healer." "Optimistic" refers to my passionate belief that we can heal and find renewed happiness. Even when a problem arises, I choose the mental high road by believing I'll overcome. "Healer" symbolizes my empathy with others and desire to facilitate their quest for personal power so they can stop their suffering. Notice that I used the word "suffering" and not "pain." Pain is inevitable in life, but suffering is optional. Suffering is the attachment we develop to our pain. But hallelujah, we can choose not to be attached to it! We're here not just to survive but to thrive, to become more and more high-functioning. One way we can do this is to extract some meaning from our suffering. We are here not just to survive the trials that have befallen us but to find our deeper purpose through them.

Crime crusader John Walsh, who lost his six-year-old son, Adam, to an unspeakable murder by a pedophile in 1981, is a prime example of this. He once confessed to me that he had come close to losing his mind during that horrible time. Instead, he and his wife, Reve, discovered their new life urge when they started the National Center for Missing and Exploited Children, as well as the popular TV show *America's Most Wanted*. There's no telling how many lives have been saved as psychopaths like the one who molested and slaughtered their child have been caught and brought to justice. As I write this, their TV show is credited with helping capture 750 felons. They distanced themselves from their suffering by responding to a stronger purpose.

When something bad happens to us, we go through predictable stages of grief, first identified by Elisabeth Kübler-Ross in her groundbreaking book, *On Death and Dying*. I once met this remarkable pioneer who has done so much to shed light on this painful subject. Elisabeth taught us that talking about death won't kill us. In fact, it can free us. The five stages of grieving she identified are *denial, anger, bargaining, depression,* and *acceptance.*

When you or I experience a loss or challenge of some kind, at first we don't want to believe it. That's denial: "This can't be happening to me!" we cry. Then we get angry and rail at God or our fellow humans: "Why me? It's not fair!" Next we enter a bargaining phase: "I'll do anything to have it go back to the way it was before." Then we get depressed as the new reality finally begins to sink in. No matter whether we deny or get angry, no matter how much we bargain, our lives have changed. In the fifth stage, we finally call a truce with the situation as it is, even though we prefer it to be different. When we evolve and choose to find some new purpose, we help ourselves move not merely to acceptance, but to transcendence. We don't just put up with the way things are, we triumph because we find our greatest meaning through it. After all, our peace of mind is the ultimate goal.

Recently I had the privilege to hostess *Lifetime's Achievement Awards: Women Changing the World,* which paid tribute to seven ordinary women who have done something extraordinary. Honoree Wynona Ward still carries vivid memories of the violence and sexual abuse she and her mother suffered at the hands of her father. Originally a truck driver, Wynona eventually put herself through law school. She now runs a free legal service called Have Justice—Will Travel. She not only represents battered women in court, but visits clients who might otherwise have no way of getting to lawyers or social services, by traveling hundreds of miles a week on the backroads of her home state of Vermont.

Like me, like John Walsh, Wynona Ward found renewed purpose in the very thing that was her greatest challenge. She healed and helped others. You can too. You're no different from John, Wynona, and me. You can keep your challenge from becoming your tombstone. You can use your dilemma as your stepping-stone to enlightenment. Think about the woman who started Mothers Against Drunk Drivers (MADD) after the death of her daughter to a drunk driver. Since MADD's creation, the number of deaths caused by inebriated drivers has gone down every year! You too can transform your suffering by finding a new life purpose.

And where are we meant to be shining, and by whom is our shining required? —AMOS OZ

Finding Purpose

You won't find your purpose by asking for directions from the guy at the gas station. Purpose is found when each of us comes to understand our gifts and passions (see Choice #9) and what deeply matters to us, given the sufferings of our lives. Where do you want to make a difference? Where do you want to aim your talents?

Each and every one of us wants to know that our life matters, that there is a reason for our existence. A friend's outgoing phone message is "Tell me who you are and what you want." If you pause to consider these questions in metaphysical terms, they are the ultimate, thought-provoking questions: *Who are you? What do you want?* These questions can't be easily answered; they can only be explored and learned from as we ask them over and over again.

One way to begin understanding how to live out our purpose every day is by writing a personal mission statement. A mission statement identifies your priorities and points you in the direction you wish to go. It's your own personal commitment to yourself regarding what you wish to be doing. It helps you decide what to add or subtract from your daily activities so that you come closer to fulfilling your mission. Companies create mission statements—why not you?

Here's what I came up with: "My mission is to slow down, simplify, and be kind so that I can help alleviate suffering and promote happiness in other people—particularly women—through self-awareness." In order for me to create this statement, it was crucial for me to know my values—what I want and what really matters to me. Once I had my mission, I began to consider it in my decision making. It helps me navigate through my choice making.

For instance, it's part of my mission to slow down and simplify so that I can be more aware of every moment as it unfolds. I intend to be 100 percent present while every precious minute is happening. That's why I've written this book the old-fashioned way—by hand. I can't imagine typing my thoughts on a typewriter. I enjoy the slow, deliberate process and the sound of a pencil on a clean, fresh sheet of paper. Believe it or not, I don't use a cell phone and I am a virgin when it comes to computers. Although I'm hip to what's out there, I just prefer simple.

Part of my mission to savor ordinary moments and everyday pleasures arose from my coming to terms with the limited energy inflicted by hepatitis C and realizing how short and unpredictable life really is. Now I stop, look, and listen . . . feel, smell, taste, and touch. I put all my attention onto savoring the sensory experiences of the present moment. I rarely talk on the phone. I'm a face-to-face person. You can't hug or hold the hand of an e-mail, phone, or fax. (I do, however, have a designated phone line, called "the mom line," with a specific ring so Wy and Ash can reach me twenty-four hours a day.) America is a touch-deprived culture, but you'd never know it when you're around me! I thrive on bear hugs and smiling faces.

To stick to my mission, I consciously limit what media I watch, read, or listen to. I sometimes go on media fasts to protect my sanity from the world's insanity.

To stay true to my mission, I also vigilantly "just say no to clutter." To keep organized, I answer correspondence as soon as I receive it. I call to cancel junk mail. If I buy something, I try to get rid of something else. I've chosen to live in a modest, two-bedroom house with a carport so I can better manage it. Voluntary simplicity is not depriving. It's the exact opposite. I like to be "free to be." Success isn't stuff, it's people. It's enjoying what you have. I plan my schedule very carefully, because if I don't watch it my day is gone faster than the speed of life! I don't prioritize my schedule anymore. I just schedule my priorities.

As far as the rest of my mission statement—being kind and helping to alleviate suffering and promote happiness—well, that's partly what I am doing writing this book. Like the Dalai Lama, who said, "My religion is simple. My religion is kindness," I'm practicing my religion. I take the word "kindness" to mean to treat like kin. I want you to be happy and healthy enough to enjoy the minutes in your day.

Wy learned the benefits of a mission statement too. One day after 9/11, she declared, "Mom, my mission as an entertainer is to use my music for good. I feel we should go to a military base and entertain the troops." So off we went to Fort Campbell, Kentucky, to the 101st Airborne, to perform a concert to encourage and thank the young men and women going off to Kandahar, Afghanistan, to fight the Taliban. It was an unbelievably moving day. Holding hands in a circle in the hangar, I led the departing soldiers in a prayer for their safety. Then Wy and I hugged them and their families as they said their farewells. Their commander and now three-star general Dick Cody (whose son Clint was in Kandahar, too) saluted them as they boarded the transport aircraft for the twenty-hour flight to a foreign land. General Cody's parting words: "God bless you as you fulfill your 'mission' to protect our nation's safety."

Only a few months later, at a World Leadership Conference in Dublin, Ireland, I found myself seated next to Hamid Karzai, the leader of the freedom movement in Afghanistan. He shared his story of finding his mission. Distraught at the suffering that Osama bin Laden had caused in his country, he had found three like-minded men, a cell phone, and two motorcycles, and led the revolution to return his people to freedom.

People like General Cody and Hamid Karzai understand their mission in life, which allows them to live with more satisfaction and intention. They have found a strong life urge by knowing where they want to take a stand.

You are only as powerful as that for which you stand. Do you stand for more money in the bank and a bigger house? Do you stand for an attractive mate? Do you stand for imposing your way of thinking upon others? These are the stands of the personality seeking to satisfy its wants. Do you stand . . . for the beauty and compassion of each soul? Do you stand for forgiveness and humbleness? These are the stands of the personality that has aligned itself with soul. This is the position of a truly powerful personality. —GARY ZUKAV

Your Turn Now

Have you discovered your purpose? I believe that you and I stand up for what we stand for. In Hollywood, I see that too many people who don't stand for anything will fall for anything. As someone has said, "It is better to light a candle than curse the darkness." A mission statement is a way to light that candle.

To begin to think about your purpose, answer the following questions:

- When was the last time that you stood up for something? What was involved? How did it make you feel?

- Who inspires you?

- Who angers you? What upsets you most about the world that you would change if you could?

- What excites you most about life?

- What talents could you put to use? (Examples: love of animals, skill at organizing, a flair for poster making.)

- What dreams of contribution do you have? How do you want to make a difference in the world?

Now, armed with the answers to these questions, you're ready to make your personal mission statement. There are many ways to do it. A good one is by Laurie Beth Jones, which is described in her book *The Path*. She explains that a mission statement has three parts.

1   Choose three action words (verbs), because a mission is about action you are willing to take. (Mine were *slow down, simplify,* and *be kind.* Other examples: *teach, create, accomplish, discover, understand, play,* and *improve.*) Whatever your three verbs are, they must inspire you. One way to get at these is to ask those around you what verbs you are always using. Another is to look at the list in *The Path.*

2   Next ask yourself, "What do I stand for?" This must be something that you are willing to devote your life to. It could be something that has come out of the suffering of your life—such as eliminating abuse because you were abused—or it could be a value of yours that has always been strong: excellence or uniqueness, for instance. Whatever it is, it must be something that really matters to you. (My answer was *alleviating suffering and promoting happiness through self-awareness.*)

3   Since a mission is ultimately about helping others as well as ourselves, consider: "Who have you come to help? Who

or what do you deeply care about?" (My answer was *people, particularly women,* because my heart goes out to all the women on welfare who are suffering the way I did when I was a struggling single mother.) What cause touches your heart the most? Children? The elderly? Those in war-torn countries? Racism? Hunger? The homeless? It doesn't have to be a group of people. It could be the environment, animal abuse, education, alternate energy—whatever you wish to focus parts one and two on. The more specific you can be, the more focused your subsequent actions will be.

Then you put the three parts together into one sentence. Here are some examples:

- "My mission is to foster, support, and encourage the uniqueness of every human being."

- "My mission is to defend, protect, and safeguard the beauty of the natural world."

- "My mission is to teach, nurture, and encourage youth at risk."

Now that you have a sense of your personal mission, are there things you need to change in your daily life in order to enact it? Over 150 years ago Henry David Thoreau said, "Our life is frittered away by detail. . . . Simplify, simplify, then simplify some more." This is even more relevant today. Are you living in a kingdom of stuff? Are your laborsaving devices freeing you up, or do you sometimes feel like a slave to them?

A girlfriend's grandmother came to visit at my friend's new home. Sitting in the kitchen surrounded by a variety of the latest appliances, she had to ask, "Grandma, if you could have only one modern convenience, which would you pick?" Grandmother answered thoughtfully, "Running water." Join me in getting back to basics so that you have time to enjoy your days and nights.

> *Make out a list of four things you're currently*
> *spending most of your money on (home, car, clothing,*
> *schooling . . .). Then make a list of your four favorite*
> *ways to spend time. Any overlapping? Are you living*
> *for material goods, or for the good of yourself and those*
> *you love? Do you spend so much time every day making*
> *a living that you're not living your purpose?*

Once we understand our mission, our reason for living, we can make better choices. And you will be surprised how, when you find that newer, stronger life urge, the universe will line up and help you. Here's a quote by Henry David Thoreau to inspire you on this quest: *"If one advances confidently in the direction of his dreams and remembers to live the life he has imagined, he will meet with a success unexpected in common hours."*

Asking for help does not mean that we are weak
or incompetent. It usually indicates an advanced
level of honesty and intelligence. —ANNE WILSON SCHAEF

18 You and I May Not Have It All Together, but Together We Can Have It All

One of the greatest gifts from my career in country music was the rewards of friendship. During the twenty years of raising Wy and Ashley alone, my days and nights were consumed with providing food, clothing, shelter, and TLC. I experienced tremendous loneliness. I had no time or energy for friends and lived too far from family. There was even an estrangement period of about six years when Mom and I didn't communicate at all.

That all changed dramatically once I began touring. On the road, the band and crew became my extended family. I looked forward to seeing the fans' familiar faces in every town. Inside the industry, I developed close girlfriends like Tammy Wynette and Reba McEntire. We bonded over the unique requirements and ups and downs of stardom. Suddenly I found myself surrounded by people twenty-four/seven. I had contact on a daily basis with more people than the average person meets in a month. I was energized by others' stories and constantly inspired by our interactions. This network of relationships was a powerful, life-enhancing force.

Then I got sick. As I lay alone in my darkened bedroom at home one day, suddenly the fear of isolation from this marvelous network engulfed me. It also began to occur to me that I'd always been the one to whom others came for help, advice, comfort. Now I was indeed "the friend in need."

I began feeling as if I had been unplugged from life support. Having been Elvis's backup singer, Larry had witnessed firsthand how celebrities can wall themselves off not just from outsiders, but from personal relationships. Elvis hadn't reached out as he began to decline. As I faced down death, I refused to let that happen to me. My experiences on the road had taught me how important a support system was for my mental and emotional well-being. To survive this physical crisis, I had to draw on all the help I could find. Quickly I began to make Choice #18: YOU AND I MAY NOT HAVE IT ALL TOGETHER, BUT TOGETHER WE CAN HAVE IT ALL.

I began by circling the wagons and calling in the cavalry. I found a therapist in whose presence I broke the news of the actual prognosis to Larry. I summoned a prayer healing with the elders of our church. I surrendered my pride and allowed Wy and Ash to see I was vulnerable and uncertain, which allowed them to feel needed.

Then, after watching the Bill Moyers special *Healing and the Mind,* I made a hit list of experts to consult. I checked out the brainiacs that Bill featured on that series, met with them, and began incorporating their recommendations into my everyday routine. As I met with these medical scientists, I felt a growing sense of camaraderie. It was the same sense of belonging I felt around fellow songwriters and musicians. I wasn't going to be in this alone!

It was during this search for information on the way people heal and support that I attended a lecture by Dr. Mona Lisa Schulz. Afterward, I took her to dinner so I could question her about how to use intuition to access my body's own healing powers. We hit it off, she shared her own story of chronic illness, and now she's a regular visitor to my farm. Her counsel and friendship have been integral in my support system.

No one is wise enough by himself. —TITUS MACCIUS PLAUTUS

Separate and Sick

You and I don't do well alone. I uncovered studies showing that women who feel alone and isolated succumb to breast and ovarian cancer at several times the normal, expected rate. College students who report cold and distant relationships with parents (especially moms) have early onset of hypertension and may develop heart disease decades later. Women with smaller social networks give birth to smaller babies. Heart attack survivors who live by themselves die at twice the rate of those who live with other people. Got your attention?

Dr. David Spiegel at Stanford followed eighty-six advanced breast cancer patients, fifty of whom joined a small support group that met every Friday as part of their treatment. Eighteen months later, a third of those receiving the extra social support in the group setting were still alive—yet every one of the others had passed away.

The well-documented Roseto Study, about the power of support, is one of the most paradoxical. Until 1965, this small town in eastern Pennsylvania had residents who smoked, ate red meat, drank, and had other unhealthy habits. Yet residents of nearby Bangor who also smoked, ate, drank, and relied on the same doctors and hospitals had a much higher death rate from heart attacks. The difference was discovered to be Roseto's tightly knit social life. This close community had been founded in 1882 by southern Italian immigrants and often had three-generation households. There was a strong commitment to their faith as well as family ties. This study established that the benefits of religious ties and strong support systems can override even unhealthy habits.

Research also shows that married people live longer than singles. I don't think I would have made it if I hadn't had Larry by my side. He also became my prayer warrior. Obviously people who have companionship have someone available to share their feelings with and remind them to take their meds, go to the doctor, and eat and rest properly. Rehabs count on group support to help patients make a healthier change. Eighty percent of all lifestyle changes will fail without a support system. (I guess even a happy hour is a form of support group, although not a healthy one.) To make lasting changes, it is essential that you create and maintain a good support system.

You have to do it by yourself, and you can't do it alone.
—MARTIN RUTTE

Good Repair

A good friend is one of the greatest supports we can have in our lives. Having a true friend is like sitting together on a swing for an hour, not saying a word, and then coming away believing that it was the best conversation you ever had. One of the many important lessons I learned from my hard times is the importance of friend maintenance. Because I'm away from home so much and around people all the time, when I am at the farm I'm happy to stay put. I dig in like a flea on a hound. Larry complained that we hadn't developed enough couples relationships. So we consciously built our network of several couples. Paul and Dez and Merlin and Eilene gather under the big shade tree in our backyard on Saturday nights for what we call "The World According to Us" discussions. Eilene and Merlin were even married under this tree, now called "the wedding tree." During their ceremony, Wy sang; then Grace and Elijah rang the big wind chimes hanging from the tree, because they sound like church bells. You don't have to go out or spend a lot of money to have good times.

A girlfriend credits one of the reasons she's been happily married for almost thirty years to the fact that she and her husband have a date night several times a month. She goes out with her girlfriends and he goes out with the guys! And Larry and his best friend, Dominick, have poker nights.

Ash has the strongest network of girlfriends I know of. She has gal pals from out of town at her farm for a week, and they indulge in all things girly. When Ashley's movie *Divine Secrets of the Ya-Ya Sisterhood* inspired women across America to celebrate sisterhood in spectacular fashion, Wy and I took nine girlfriends from our dentist's office to see it for a big girls' night out. I predict it will be a cult hit as it celebrates the richness of long-term friendships.

Who's your oldest friend? Do you have friends of different ages? The love of friends is good for us—body, mind, and soul. When I'm with my friends from childhood, I'm stirred by feelings of love, appreciation, and understanding. We chastise one another when one of us is stuck in negative or irrational thinking. Since we have a long personal history, we can point out times when the other survived a crisis. We do constructive, supportive activities such as exercising and walking together. There's a group of older gals I know of who walk laps inside a mall regularly. They call themselves "The Brazen Huskies." Exercising with friends helps us stay with the workout. We let our hair down and relax together with our buddies. I do my "geek goddess act" and perform my notorious "big butt" dance only in front of "hens." (Never mind!)

Shared joy is double joy, and shared sorrow is half sorrow.
—SWEDISH PROVERB

Four-Legged, Winged, Gilled, or Feathered Friends

Support comes in all shapes and sizes. If you're one of the 58 million cat owners or 53 million dog owners, you won't need statistics to prove the benefits of being a pet lover. My constant canine companion, Tilly, is in my lap as I write this.

But behavioral scientists know for sure that people who care for pets recover faster from illness. Pets lift our spirits, help us be more optimistic, and give us a purpose through being responsible for them. They supply us unconditional love, support, and companionship. The tactile stimulation of petting an animal reduces blood pressure and stimulates relaxation. Even watching fish in an aquarium can lower blood pressure. The nonjudgmental silence of pets encourages us to communicate and release our worries. I say a life without pets is like eating but not being able to taste.

Dogs think they're human. Cats think they're gods.
Dogs have owners, cats have staffs. —ANONYMOUS

Geniuses Have
Good Taste in Ideas

Support comes in all shapes, sizes, and colors. There's support for your mind, your body, your soul. One law of physics states, "Like attracts like." As we get our act together by figuring out what we want and discovering that we are lovable, we begin to attract people with healthier self-esteem and better boundaries.

I know. The more work I did on myself, the more high-quality people entered my support system. Along the way, I consciously sought out those who saw things in me that I was not aware of and who helped me to grow. In other words, mentors. Got any?

After I got straight with myself, I wasn't interested in ex-cons on heroin. I felt it was important to hang around someone who could teach me something valuable, someone intellectually challenging. But I never really had a mentor until I met Leon Lederman, Ph.D. We're the consummate odd couple—a hillbilly and a genius. I call him E=mc² and he refers to me as Red. In 1993, at a think tank with lots of Nobel Prize laureates, Pulitzer Prize winners, and general eggheads, I felt completely out of my league. What the heck was I going to have in common with these intellectuals, let alone contribute? Ever have that feeling?

When I met Leon and his lovely wife, Ellen, we quickly realized that the shortest distance between people is laughter! He's a wannabe comedian who won the Nobel Prize in physics in the eighties, ran Fermilab, discovered Doppler radar, and was one of the architects of the Super Collider. Oh my gosh!

In school I was so intimidated by the hard sciences that I'd get a stomachache or headache before class. Kindly Professor Leon has gracefully demystified and reframed science in such a way that now I'm intrigued by the search for answers to the mysteries of our universe. Yet, even as he exposes me to fascinating new ideas, my relationship with Leon is far more than just learning about theories of creation, neutrinos, or black holes. Leon encourages my self-confidence by saying, "Red, you're just as smart as anybody else." Leon even inspired me to write a song Wy and I recorded called "The Big Bang Boogie." I dedicated it to him and some of my other Nobel Laureate physicist pals, like Bill Phillips, Ph.D. Leon travels the world lecturing, but when he comes here to the farm, he rides horses and four-wheelers, and Ash even beat him once in a game of Trivial Pursuit (her real claim to fame).

My friendship with Leon proves that the more you and I work on ourselves, the more wonderful people will appear in our lives to join our circle of support. It's synchronicity. If, when I was thirty, someone had told me I would have a Nobel Prize–winning scientist as a friend, I'd have told him to take his medication!

Just as despair can come to one only from other human beings, hope, too, can be given to one only by other human beings.
—ELIE WIESEL

Come in Unity = Community

Despite all this evidence that we need one another, people are feeling more isolated and lonely than ever before in history. Things are changing so rapidly that few people have even remained in the same job ten years, let alone lived in the same house or neighborhood. We have larger houses but more broken homes. The electronic media have replaced our hometowns. Sociologists say that you and I need a minimum number of social contacts every week to stay sane. They've found that unless we interact with a minimum of seven people weekly, we're at risk for mental illness. People who feel isolated have a seven to ten times' higher chance of premature death or disease compared to folks who have a sense of connection to their community.

Traveling across America border to border and coast to coast, I've seen firsthand that we're living in a transient, disposable culture. One afternoon Wy and I were enjoying Americana up front on our bus as we noticed a woman pull into her garage. As she hit the garage opener and disappeared from sight, she never looked toward homes on the left or right. That's when Wy and I observed that there were no sidewalks or porches in this neighborhood. It was striking that although we can send a man and woman into outer space, we no longer walk across the street to meet our neighbors. You and I can take back our neighborhoods by paying attention to what's going on.

In my childhood neighborhood, I knew everyone. I sold Girl Scout Cookies by myself door to door. I trick-or-treated at every house and often went inside. I safely played all over our neighborhood. I walked unescorted to all the schools I attended.

An area of constant concern to me is that real people are underrepresented in the media. My friendly hometown of Ashland, Kentucky, is thankfully still a front-porch town. Some of the dear souls who live there have indoor-outdoor carpeting on their porches, pillows in the glider swings, plants, magazine racks, and sometimes even portable phones. When I visit Mom, I put on my most comfortable walking shoes and strike out in all directions. Walking down Hilton Avenue one summer's eve, I came upon an eighty-year-old couple, the McKenzies, who invited me to join them on their porch for a glass of iced tea. Over the next hour, I experienced the timelessness and hospitality of folks who understand the art of being in the moment.

Inner peace begins at home. Larry and I share a peaceful valley with our daughters, son-in-law, and our two grandchildren. We've collectively chosen to live in an underpopulated rural area with a slower beat and rhythm. It nourishes each of us as an individual, as well as our family life. It promotes a strong sense of neighborliness. For example, a week after 9/11, we all worked together to put on a commemorative musical evening and rally to raise money for the Survivors Fund. As I spoke about patriotism and led the prayer from Marty and Bruce Hunt's rambling front porch, I gazed out over hundreds of friendly faces who'd gathered there in unity. Trucks and cars were parked in the field across the road with cattle. Kids and dogs played in the side meadows. The totality of that scene represented everything that's still right about this great nation. My sadness was somewhat assuaged, and I felt hopeful.

The past is a foreign country. They do things differently there.
—ANONYMOUS

Your Turn Now

Take a good look at your support system—individuals, neighbors, and community.

- Who could you call at two in the morning to bail you out of jail?

- When was the last time you had a night out with friends? Have you been so involved in work that you have not been maintaining your friendships?

- Are you facing a specific issue for which you could use a support group's influence?

- Do you and your significant other have couples to hang out with?

- Let your passions lead you to like-minded people and developing a hobby. I had a middle-aged girlfriend who began taking tap-dancing lessons. It fulfilled an old dream; she also lost twenty pounds and made new friends.

- Culture vultures live longer. Start going out more to concerts, lectures, museums; join a book discussion group.

- How about forming your own group? I started a monthly book discussion group at our mom-and-pop bookstore in Franklin to discuss holistic healing. It's been going strong four years now. I know a group of wives of Nashville songwriters who call themselves the "La Las" and meet every Thursday for lunch.

- Interested in grassroots social activism? Do you even know your neighbors? Create a community group in your neighborhood. For instance, our rural school started a Kids Onstage program to encourage musical talents in shy and underprivileged kids.

- Who do you admire, and why? Take my lead and muster your courage to seek out people in the field of your interest.

- Get rid of energy vampires and hang out with people who replenish, encourage, and inspire you.

- Consider getting a pet, even a fish.

- Read biographies and watch TV and movies about people who've got their act together. You'll be amazed how much you have in common. The company you keep determines the opportunities you meet.

Remember—you and I may not have it all together, but together we can have it all!

19 Develop the Eight Characteristics of a Survivor Personality

I wanted to live. So I set out seeking ways to survive my death sentence. My crisis presented opportunity as well as danger as I chose the opportunity to explore new dimensions in medicine. In this quest, I discovered Choice #19: DEVELOP THE EIGHT CHARACTERISTICS OF A SURVIVOR PERSONALITY. My therapist presented psychological evidence that survivors of difficulties, whether emotional, physical, or circumstantial, all seem to display eight specific characteristics. They are (1) a strong spiritual belief, (2) a strong support system, (3) a sense of humor, (4) a connection to nature, (5) goals and a purpose to work toward, (6) good nutrition, (7) regular exercise and rest, (8) an open belief system.

I was already incorporating most of these critical lifestyle choices and enthusiastically began to explore number eight. Some characteristics have whole chapters devoted to them. But because each is so important to general happiness, health, and well-being, as we come to the end of our journey I'll explain how I wove each into my daily routine. After all, they are the reason I'm cured. They are now my source of guidance as I face all conflicts and challenges. And it is my hope that they will become resources for you as well, whatever your circumstances.

Some words of clarification as we begin. There can always be healing, but there may not always be a cure. The word "healing" means making whole. As a nurse, I witnessed many of my patients in the hospital who, despite disease or injury, experienced wholeness. Then, as a patient myself, I met countless others who remain whole: content and wiser in spite of their difficulties. Self-awareness and spiritual growth through achieving a state of acceptance can result in even a terminally ill patient's being at peace, no matter how long his or her life is.

Until I experienced this phenomenon myself, I didn't get it. I would hear people say that being diagnosed with cancer was the best thing that had ever happened to them. I figured the disease process must have clouded their mind. Yet strangely enough, I also came to see how illness and tragedy can be our greatest teachers. They provide the opportunity for personal growth that can awaken us to living more fully. A calamity can bring you face-to-face with whatever's not working in your life. Remember, your body takes over when you've refused to emotionally acknowledge what's bothering you. "Spontaneous remission" doesn't necessarily mean a cure. This medical term refers to a sudden, unexpected lessening or abating of symptoms over time.

Ultimately what matters is how much life there is in your life. These eight characteristics might help in curing what ails you; they certainly can be healing.

It is not the adversity in our circumstance, it is how we interpret the adversity. It's how we consciously choose to cope and adapt that determines our physical, emotional and spiritual health.
—BLAIR JUSTICE, PH.D.

---

1. A Strong Spiritual Belief

This one was natural for me. Having explored all the world's major religions, I've chosen Jesus Christ to be my personal mentor, teacher, and savior. I have an unshakable faith as a Christian. To strengthen my scriptural optimism, I began using what Jesus advocated about praying the answer instead of the problem. This relates to neuroscientific data about how we can reframe all our thoughts to create a positive feedback loop in brain circuitry. Whenever I felt doubt and despair creeping in, I would step out of my circumstances and claim my healing and (possibly) a cure. When we know not to complain to God how big our problem is, but describe to our problem how big God is, we reverse the curse. We create a positive expectation, and our body begins believing and fulfilling what we are saying. In prayer, I would *Praise, Repent, Ask,* and *Yield.* Thus, I declared the Lord to be my doctor, and my family, friends, and fans my medicine.

You and I are spiritual beings having a human experience here on earth. The universe runs on spiritual laws, and every problem has a spiritual solution. Whatever your beliefs are, I encourage you to find comfort and inspiration in them and to express them in your everyday activities. Religion is usually a result of geography and familial influences. AA says that religion is for people who are afraid of hell and spirituality is for people who've already been through hell. Discovering your spiritual self will allow you to have a more clarified set of values as well as a deeper appreciation of why we're here. Life's challenges bring us face-to-face with the source of our creation and the realization that there is a divine plan for us.

*If there is no God, nothing matters. If there is a God,
nothing else matters.* —ANONYMOUS

2. A Strong Support System

I've discussed in Chapter 18 the importance of a support system
and how I rallied family and friends around me when I got sick.
Looking back, I realized I had seen this phenomenon at work
when I was an RN. Whenever I'd walk into a room where there
were two women with the same diagnosis and prognosis, I'd feel
better about the healing potential of the one who had visitors,
cards, flowers, and phone calls.

You don't have to be sick to benefit from loving concern. A
death in the family, divorce, a job loss—all human challenges are
easier with caring people by your side. That's because positive
gestures of support increase the production of opiates in your
brain, those feel-good chemicals that flow throughout your body
and improve your overall sense of emotional and spiritual well
being. A strong support network is the best life insurance any
person can have.

It is in the shelter of each other that the people live.
—IRISH PROVERB

3. A Sense of Humor

I laughed out loud when I found out that the third characteristic of survivors is humor! I'm living proof that she who laughs, lasts. The Judd family takes laughter and having fun seriously. Perhaps it's in our DNA, because we seem to instinctively know laughter is good for us. Our family revels in game night, when we play interactive board games like Cranium, Scattergories, Taboo, and Trivial Pursuit. We jokers are wild!

Humor is a release of optimism, resiliency, creativity, and endurance. When you can laugh at life's absurdities, it helps put you in the driver's seat, gives you more of a sense of being in control. It's also life's shock absorber. As Victor Borge noted, "Laughter is the shortest distance between two people." When my doctor told me I had to go to the admitting office at the hospital, I fired off, "OK, but I ain't admitting to nothing." We both enjoyed a brief moment of relief and instantly felt a connection.

Laughter can be like changing a baby diaper. It may not be permanent, but it sure makes the situation better temporarily. Those who can laugh at themselves and their mistakes will never cease to be amused. It's no laughing matter that the average preschooler laughs about four hundred times a day, yet the average adult laughs only fifteen times a day—unless you are a Judd or are around a Judd!

The scientific backup citing the benefits of laughter began coming in 1976 after author Norman Cousins described how he used laughter to deal with his chronic progressive disease of the spine. Laboratory studies prove that laughter reduces stress, decreases epinephrine and norepinephrine, lowers blood pressure (thereby boosting your immune system), increases the oxygen exchange rate, decreases pain and anxiety, and stimulates the feel-good brain chemicals, the beta-endorphins.

Do you laugh often and freely? When was the last time you did the bent-over-double belly laugh? Who's the funniest person you know?

A merry heart doeth good like a medicine. —PROVERBS 17:22

---

4. A Connection to Nature

I wasn't at all surprised to discover that the survivor personality enjoys a strong connection to the natural world. Nature is a balm to all wounds. When I was too ill to walk outside, I would have Larry bundle me into his truck for a drive in the country. Being outside in the natural world reminds us that we're but a speck of sand, which helps put our problems in perspective. G.O.D.—great outdoors—feels like nature's cathedral. The sights, sounds, smells, and textures also engage the senses and help to draw you out of self-absorption. When I feel like I'm in decline, it's rejuvenating to be surrounded by growth. I also find comfort in being reminded that humans run on cycles, like the tides of the ocean, phases of the moon, or seasons of the earth. There are seasons of our souls: autumn, the time of centering; winter, the season of emptying; spring, the time of grounding; summer, the season of connecting.

Unfortunately, nowadays some people's closest connection to the natural world is as a couch potato, watching National Geographic or the Travel Channel—or even worse, a reality show like *Survivor*. Modern humans are becoming more and more removed from the wonders and solace of the natural environment. The irony is, the more technology we come up with, the more you and I need to be outdoors. Our sedentary society sits in offices all day, stews inside cars in traffic all the way home, and then plunks down in front of TV or the computer. Not me! Join me in getting out of the bleachers of spectatorship and into the active game of spending time outside.

Do you walk in your neighborhood? Do you go to a park? What outdoor activities do you enjoy? If you are facing some difficulty, be sure to get out in nature so your connection to Mother Earth can help replenish you.

The best remedy for those who are afraid, lonely or unhappy is to go outside, somewhere where they can be quiet, alone with the heavens, nature and God. Because only then does one feel that all is as it should be and that God wishes to see people happy, amidst the simple beauty of nature. . . . I firmly believe that nature brings solace in all troubles.

—Anne Frank, during her two years of hiding in a Dutch attic

5. Goals

When you're determined to survive your hardships, it's imperative to find a goal and then focus on it. When catastrophe or disease strikes, it throws a monkey wrench into all parts of your existence. You can't work, play, or communicate as you once did. Your self-image and the ways in which you were contributing to your family and work take a blow. Figuring out some goal to work toward creates forward movement and allows you to feel less frantic about your circumstances. It gives you more of a sense of being in control in the unknown.

It may even prolong or save your life. There are documented cases of patients willing themselves to live long enough to meet a specific goal, like attending a daughter or son's wedding or graduation, or seeing a birth, or having a loved one reach the bedside for final good-byes. Everybody needs something to look forward to.

This is what I had in mind as I planned the Farewell Tour. I wanted to live long enough for Wy and me to transition from being the Judds to her initiation as a solo performer. My goal was not only to guide her through that painful process, but to be standing at the bottom of the steps to celebrate her victorious first solo outing. The myriad of details involved in planning this humungous farewell in every major city in the United States motivated me to rally. I was also determined to be there for Ashley as she set her own career plan into action and began attending auditions. Channeling creative energies kept my mind off my aches and pains and inspired me to visualize better days to come.

Goals are dreams with deadlines. —ANONYMOUS

6. Good Nutrition

You and I are living organisms, dependent upon the same resources as every other living being: nutrition, sunlight, water, shelter, and TLC. What we put into our body and how we care for it daily determines the status of our health. When we are under stress from physical or emotional challenges, it is even more important than usual to eat well. Stress depletes the body of vitamins and other nutrients. Your immune system doesn't need any extra wear and tear. When you open your refrigerator, consider it a medicine cabinet. Let fresh, healthy food be the medicine of your future.

It's not only what you eat but what's eating you. If you're ill or are struggling with something difficult, you feel out of control and scared. Understanding the importance of the healing effects of good nutrition gives you something constructive to focus on immediately. The good news is that it's not too late to repair some damage! For instance, *The Journal of the American Medical Association* states that women who consume as little as eight ounces of fish a week cut their risk of suffering a stroke almost in half. Fish do not contain much fat, and the omega-3 fatty acids found in fish are good for you. They cut down clot formations in your blood vessels and lower your triglycerides, another detrimental fatty substance found in the blood. Replacing red meat with fish like salmon and sardines also decreases high blood pressure and allows your blood vessels to become more flexible. Isn't that a "heartening" conclusion?

A century ago, Americans got what they needed on their fork in the way of nutrients. Today, with soil depletion, processing, pollutants, and added stress, you and I get less than a third of our minimum daily requirements. That's why I turn to vitamins, minerals, and supplements every day and especially when I get sick. I'm amused at how many people don't understand that vitamins are not food, but minute nutrients found inside food. When it comes to vitamins, thirteen's your lucky number: nine that are water soluble (B_1, B_2, B_3, B_5, B_6, B_{12}, biotin, folic acid, and C) and four that are fat soluble (A, D, E, and K). They must be taken with real food so they're metabolized. Minerals and supplements are each a different category.

Please realize that herbs, vitamins, and minerals cannot address underlying disease processes. And they can be potent! Be sure to discuss everything you're taking with your doctor.

Don't be one of the 60 percent of patients who don't discuss vitamins, minerals, supplements, and herbs with their physicians.

Wean yourself off foods and drinks you know aren't good for you. Your body needs to become a more efficient machine. Avoid artificial sweeteners, aspartame, and dyes. As a coffee aficionado, I began using half regular/half decaf flavored coffee in the morning and also cut back to two cups. If you drink sodas, clear sodas are better for you than dark sodas. Fresh fruit and fresh vegetables are alive with the nutrients and ingredients our body's in need of, especially when it's waging war on a disease. Cutting down on refined sugar is a no-brainer, and it also helps to reduce the risk of diabetes. Get roughage and plenty of water to facilitate regular elimination and get rid of toxins. Use a water filter, and don't drink water that tastes chlorinated.

It's a shame that more physicians don't address the role nutrition plays in prevention as well as healing, because 70 percent of all chronic diseases can be warded off with some sensible lifestyle changes. The number-one preventable cause of disease is smoking. The second most preventable is obesity.

Sixty percent of Americans are overweight or obese. Accumulating data proves that this greatly contributes to illness and premature death. Although the diet industry is a multibillion-dollar-a-year profit center, until an overweight individual addresses his or her emotional and spiritual hungers, nothing can ever satisfy them. Remember, when you're under stress, you tend to reach for harmful substances to avoid facing and dealing with your feelings. Watch out particularly for the four cravings known as CATS: caffeine, alcohol, tobacco, and sugar. If these are a problem for you, please get the help you need.

You are in charge of your state of being. You have learned to be exactly the way you are and you have the remarkable human capability to learn to be another way. Choosing ways of thinking, feeling, and doing which contribute to your health pleasures rather than your health problems is the nitty-gritty of being well.

—Ronald J. Pion

7. Regular Exercise and Rest

There are volumes of well-documented evidence that regular exercise helps you survive. Exercise is free and offers all kinds of physical and emotional benefits. It strengthens our cardiovascular systems and reduces stress. By keeping our weight down, exercise helps us maintain our appearance and therefore our self-confidence. To maintain our dignity as we age, we must not let ourselves go. Living well and looking well are the best revenge against Father Time. We're living longer, so start moving!

Despite such terrific benefits, it's mind-boggling that only one in four of us gets regular exercise. Forty percent of Americans are sedentary. But it's never too late to start, and even small changes can reap big rewards. If you're a forty-year-old female, for instance, and start taking half-hour walks today, just four days a week, you will enjoy the same benefits in warding off heart attacks as women who have exercised religiously their entire lives. Yeah!

When it comes to an exercise routine, the trick is to figure out what form of movement best suits you. Wy has a trainer and Ash runs, does yoga, and works out. When prepping for a film, she's even done strenuous kickboxing.

I've never had a personal trainer, and I'm not into going to a gym. My style is much more about stretching throughout the day and taking an evening sunset walk in my valley with Larry. Walking is the most perfect form of exercise. My grandkids offer me the chance to hike and run as we play outdoor games together. If the weather is inclement, I watch TV or read on the treadmill, which is the most popular form of exercise for females. Exercise reminds me to keep my mind where my body is. If you're like me, it's easy to live in your head, and your mind just drags your body around. After moving, I feel increased oxygen to my brain and a reduction in muscle tension. I'm more flexible and I know I'm cutting down on chances of osteoporosis by doing weight-bearing movement. Plus I feel more centered and in control of the aging process.

Two other good forms of exercise to consider, because they involve stress-reducing aspects as well as fitness ones, are yoga—a refined system of physical development focusing not only on flexibility but also on great strength, balance, and endurance—and tai chi, which is a moving form of yoga involving slow, sequential movements. Ashley loves yoga. She says, "Yoga lets me be me, comfortable and open. If I have a scene in which I'm really uptight, or if I am anxious, I like to open myself up with yoga. If you give it a chance, it will grow within you."

What form of exercise you choose matters less than doing it. Use it before you lose it.

And don't forget rest. Rest is often an overlooked priority in today's culture. Americans on average get only six and a half hours of sleep. Yet the body needs eight to nine hours of sleep per night for repairing, replicating, and re-creating cells, as well as allowing us to dream. Exercising promotes better sleep. Too often people have trouble sleeping because they haven't burned off enough stress through exercise before they lie down.

Do you awake refreshed and rested? Do you have soft, flattering light in your home? Avoid fluorescent lighting. Use candles to create a calm setting, and get a full-spectrum light machine if you are light deprived. Dim the lights in the room two hours prior to going to sleep. It helps you shut down and releases melatonin to help you sleep.

Our growing softness, our increasing lack of physical fitness is a menace to our security. —JOHN F. KENNEDY

---

8. An Open Belief System

Many patients still unfortunately look at their doctor as a deity in a lab coat in whose omniscient hands their outcome lies. Survivors, however, see their doctors as partners on their journey to wellness. They are discerning in selecting Dr. Right. They care how much a doctor knows but are just as concerned about how much he or she cares. They accept that they must be in charge in investigating every avenue toward their own healing. So they open their minds to learn all they can and consider all possible treatments.

That was certainly true for me. I am fond of saying that my door is always open and my mind is never closed. When I got sick, I opened up to learning about all the ways people can heal. As I interviewed reputable healers on my voyage of self-discovery, they became my partners in the process.

Working as an RN, although I had never heard the term "holistic medicine," I often witnessed subtle ways my patients were healing that weren't medically induced. I knew there were forces at work I couldn't explain. You can't beat modern medicine for surgical intervention, emergency trauma care, screening and testing, or antibiotics. But there are many other effective healing methods we can use for ourselves that are less intrusive, invasive, and costly.

As I've studied the research on healing for over a decade, I've come to realize the benefits of complementary techniques. I never use the term "alternative medicine" for fear of implying that it's a matter of choosing between these approaches and mainstream medicine. I can testify that both are better. I was monitoring my liver functions, getting a biopsy, and taking the drug interferon. But every night, as I drew up the interferon into the syringe, I knelt at the altar and incorporated complementary techniques. I prayed while injecting the medicine. I said aloud affirmations and used guided imagery to envision myself healthy once more. I lit a scented candle there, among my favorite souvenirs, and inhaled the aromatherapy of eucalyptus oil. I created this personalized altar to alter my thoughts. To help align my own innate healing potential, I placed on it sacred symbols such as a cross and an open Bible, and other objects that inspired me.

What we Americans call complementary is really standard practice in 80 percent of the world. Much of it, such as healing touch, scented oils, and prayer, is even written about in the Old Testament and other religious books. My dear friend the Reverend Robert Schuller even had me on his worldwide TV program, *Hour of Power,* to substantiate the scriptural authority behind these complementary measures.

The complementary techniques I will mention are those I researched before including them in my personal wellness program. There are others out there that I have not yet tried or will not recommend. I intend to write a separate book dedicated to the subject of integrated medicine.

The first effect I noticed from these techniques was a welcome sense of control. The second characteristic was an immediate lessening of my stress. The third benefit was that I was finally allowing a healthier give-and-take as I permitted myself to receive from others. The fourth was the acknowledgment that I was being treated as a whole being. Now my emotional, mental, and spiritual needs were being addressed as well as my physical ones. Too often in today's technology-driven medical world, the personality experiencing the suffering is ignored. This is why integrative medicine is also referred to as holistic. It takes into consideration the emotional, psychosocial, psychobiological, and spiritual components of the patient. Healing is an art as well as a science.

The techniques I utilized are acupuncture, affirmations, aromatherapy, biofeedback, chiropractic, massage, meditation, music, prayer, and visualization.

Acupuncture is an ancient Chinese medicine process of releasing blocked chi, or "energy life force," by the insertion of teeny disposable sterile needles into acupuncture points, known as meridians. Acupuncture is thought to inhibit pain transmissions through your nervous system, as well as releasing good endorphins. Its benefits have been studied and confirmed by the American Medical Association.

Affirmations are positive statements used to enhance healing because words are the manifestation of our thoughts. I described how I used them for emotional and mental healing in Chapter 13. When I was sick, they helped remind me that my body is a miracle and wants to heal.

Aromatherapy is gaining more recognition as a viable means of facilitating healing. Doctors at Duke University in North Carolina have discovered that there are certain smell receptors in the brain, and that certain fragrances can lower your pulse and breathing rate, which of course calms you. The sense of smell also affects the particular area of the brain that controls fear and anxiety. Lavender, rose, orange, peach, violet, and apple are soothing. Biochemistry has proven that certain scents help lift depression, promote sleep, and stimulate energy. Even now that I am well, I enjoy my scented candles, scented soaps, and bath oils. They give me a "scents of comfort."

Biofeedback is a noninvasive technique used to give people information and control over certain seemingly automatic physical processes. It has been shown to lessen the pain of migraine headaches, decrease anxiety, lessen GI disorders and heart disease, and lower blood pressure. Electronic monitors measure a patient's responses, and the patient is shown the measurements. He or she then learns how to control physical responses through the feedback loop that is created by the information. It's also used for children with ADHD to help them focus by teaching them to route thoughts through the temporal lobe. Biofeedback helped me see just how much control I do have over my physical functions.

Chiropractic involves gentle manipulation to keep your skeletal frame in alignment.

I also turned to *massage.* Touch is one of the oldest forms of healing. As early as 5000 B.C., the act of laying on of hands was practiced. Jesus, too, went about laying hands on the sick. I found that nursing home patients who get regular massages exhibit less depression and memory loss. Massage normalizes heart rate and blood pressure, raises serotonin levels, and decreases stress hormones. It relaxes tight muscles, relieves pain, and stimulates lymphatic drainage. It allows me to shut down and receive TLC.

I've personally witnessed the healing power of *music.* Music increases the amplitude of alpha brain waves and the production of pleasurable endorphins. The study of how sound waves impact us physically is entrainment. The scientific study of how music affects brain wave activity is psychoacoustics. I used the Farewell Tour as a way to give myself both forms of music therapy. Choose music that enhances your mood, whether calming and soothing or stimulating. Calm music played during meals stimulates digestion. I think crude, violent, homophobic, misogynistic gangsta rap is to music what Etch A Sketch is to art. Be careful what lyrics are feeding you subliminally.

Meditation has been shown to lower blood pressure and heart rate, and to increase the tendency to look on the bright side by increasing the activity of the left prefrontal lobes of the brain (where we experience optimism, joy, gratitude, and other positive emotions). When I use meditation for healing, I breathe in peace and breathe out power and serenity.

Meditation and prayer are different. Meditation is a form of self-contemplation centered on the self. Prayer is God centered. It is a dialogue, a conversation with God.

I have referred to *prayer* many times because I am living proof of its healing power. Spiritual isolation results in stress. Over twenty-three centuries ago, Plato warned that we can't separate our spirit from our physical body. There is ample evidence that, in the words of Harvard cardiologist Herbert Benson, "we may be wired for God." There have been over seven hundred research studies demonstrating a relationship between prayer or other spiritual practices and improved health. One study at Duke University even showed that harmful substances produced by microorganisms in the bloodstream called interleukin-6 were significantly lower in folks who attended church regularly.

If you are interested in finding out more, check out my friend Chester Tolson's new book, *The Healing Power of Prayer*, which he cowrote with Harold Koenig, M.D. I am also a big fan of Dr. Larry Dossey, who wrote *Healing Words: The Power of Prayer and the Practice of Medicine.* In our meeting in his town of

Santa Fe, New Mexico, I soaked up his 130 case studies from his forty-plus-year illustrious career of witnessing the beneficial effects of prayer in healing, including nonlocal prayer, which is prayer from a distance. I know that folks praying for me around the country made a difference in my healing.

Prayer reminds me that I belong to God and am part of the universe. Prayer not only changed things, it changed *me*. When I was sick, I had a healing prayer service at my church in which the elders laid their hands on me, anointed me with oils, and prayed for my healing. Jesus Christ's half brother James said in James 5:14–15: "Is anyone among you sick? Let him call for the elders of the church and let them pray over him, anointing him with oil in the name of the Lord. And the prayer of faith will save the sick, and the Lord will raise him up." Only God heals in faith healing and miracles. Human believers are only facilitators. As it says in Psalm 103:1–3:

> *Bless the Lord, O my soul,*
> *And all that is within me, bless His holy name!*
>
> *Bless the Lord, O my soul,*
> *And forget not all His benefits:*
>
> *Who forgives all your iniquities,*
> *Who heals all your diseases.*

Visualization is the process of visually imagining the positive state of health and happiness that you want. When I was sick, I put a picture of myself when I was a happy, healthy four-year-old in a prominent place, where I saw it every day to help me visualize the possibility of health.

I have a unique perspective, having been a member of the mainstream medical community and then finding myself a patient. As a result of what I learned and experienced, I am a health care reform advocate. As certain complementary techniques are proven effective, they should be covered by insurance. As it stands now, the "wealth care" industry needs healing. I intend to do what I can to facilitate the process. I'm proud to be associated with Dr. Andrew Weil, my close ally and America's most respected authority on integrative medicine. His goal is to see integrative techniques taught in the nation's 127 accredited medical schools.

The purpose of healing is to be in harmony within ourselves.
—O. CARL SIMONTON, M.D.

Your Turn Now

- Which of the eight characteristics of a survivor personality do you already have? Which have you not yet thought of? Can you see the benefit of these?

- Make a list of all eight characteristics and put it in a prominent place. Glance at it as you begin your day.

- Focus on the reason you want to survive. Visualize how you intend your circumstances to turn out.

- Congratulate yourself on being alive and overcoming past challenges.

- Phrase your prayer in a positive way, stating the desired outcome.

- Which complementary methods do you think would help you? Which one are you willing to commit to developing right now? To find out more about them, check into any of Dr. Andrew Weil's wonderful books or visit his website at www.drweil.com.

- What comes to mind when you hear the word "home"? How do you feel when you walk into your home?

- You might want to create your own altar that includes objects that symbolize the better parts of your life, sacred symbols that have deep meaning for you, and tokens to remind you what really matters to you.

- Identify enjoyable daily rituals that sustain and comfort you.

- Associate with people who can teach you valuable information.

- Discuss what you're learning with others. Share your story with like-minded people. Share information and references, and continue having an open mind.

The life you save may be your own.

I don't know what your destiny will be, but one thing I do know: The only ones among you who will be truly happy are those who have sought and found how to serve.

—ALBERT SCHWEITZER

20 Love Heals the Giver as Well as the Receiver

The very first stop on our Farewell Tour that winter of '91 predicted that it was going to be an extraordinary adventure. The Judds have always been about audience participation. But now, lined up around the bus after the show, were not only fans but folks dealing with all manner of illnesses and personal crises. They had heard about my hepatitis C and came to be inspired by our music, get insights into how we were handling our crises, and share their own stories.

The first one to come up on our bus, the Dream Chaser, was a middle-aged mother of several children who'd just had a radical mastectomy. Her husband had left her because he couldn't deal with her cancer. As we listened tearfully to her plight, instinctively she and I began supporting each other. This was the first time I'd ever prayed with a stranger. Are you comfortable praying with others?

Wy began calling me a "musicianary." She said, "God doesn't call the qualified, He qualifies the called." Something marvelous was happening. As I shared stories with more and more people, I saw how much we have in common. We chose to become better instead of bitter. Both sides experienced breakthroughs. I began stringing their stories together like pearls and wore this metaphorical necklace as I continued on my way. By the end of all these nightly visits, I felt recharged instead of drained. Don't get me wrong; I had some rough spells. Wy became protective of me and would sometimes lock the bus door and turn out the lights. She'd banish me to my room, help me undress, and put me in bed. Daughter, may I have a glass of water and a bedtime story? I began feeling better and better.

I'd begun applying wisdom gained from Dr. Blair Justice's groundbreaking book, *Who Gets Sick: How Beliefs, Moods, and Thoughts Affect Your Health*. Besides the Bible, it's the most influential book I've ever read. As Wy and I headed for Houston, Texas, to perform at the Astrodome, my head was swimming with questions for Dr. Justice. When I called his office at the University of Texas to invite him to our show, he had no idea who the Judds even were. Dr. J thought I was a judge! When I told him who I was and what we did, he asked incredulously, "If you have hepatitis, how in the world do you think you're going to be able to stand, let alone perform?" But this doctor makes bus calls. As Blair and his psychologist wife, Rita, stepped onto our bus after watching our show, Blair shook his finger under my nose and, with a sly grin, teased, "I know exactly what you are doing out there, missy. You're absorbing the energy from those thousands of supportive fans and your passion for music and communicating to boost your body's beleaguered immune system." Busted! He labeled me "The Body of Evidence."

As we settled in to discuss the information in his book, Blair continued, "I only wish I'd known about your situation earlier, so I could've included a chapter on you in my book." As a researcher, he was quite curious about details of my daily routine and particularly what happened to me while I was onstage.

I explained how much I love living in America and how I thrived on the daily stimulation of waking up on our bus in a different city and meeting all types of people. Living in our traveling home with Wy and our dogs, Loretta Lynn and Banjo, with frequent visits from Ashley and Larry, kept me comforted by the love of family. The band, crew, and fans were our neighbors. I was grounded by nightly rituals to give me structure: putting on makeup, bonding with Wynonna while she did my hair, dressing up in my fantasy stage outfit. When we're in transition, rituals become so important for centering. Besides that, the exhilarating walk to the stage always fills me with excitement and joy!

Blair explained that these acts of movement and being in control, plus the celebratory gratification of how hard I'd worked to accomplish this career, gave me a flush of the feel-good neuropeptides like dopamine and serotonin. These not only were making me feel better emotionally but concurrently were greatly stimulating my struggling immune system.

Music was not only stimulating my immune system, it was helping my relationship with Wy. For music not only brought Wy and me together in the first place, it allowed our relationship to continue the healing process during our career together. In this last beneficial stage, it was allowing us to cut our psychological umbilical cord so that we could individuate. We became closer than ever because my illness forced each of us to open her mind and heart to what mattered most.

In planning the Farewell Tour, I also expected that connecting with the fans would be a great source of emotional support. I've always appreciated the symbiotic relationship I had with the Judd fans and see myself in them. These people had changed my life for the better, so I wanted them to know emphatically how much they mean to me. It was while going through all this that the next choice was revealed, Choice #20: LOVE HEALS THE GIVER AS WELL AS THE RECEIVER! The more you and I choose to give of ourselves, the more we will receive—in loving connections and therefore in therapeutic boosts to our immune systems.

Health is an intuitive perception of the universe as being of one fabric. Health is maintaining communication with the animals and plants and minerals and stars. It is knowing death and life and knowing no difference. It is blending and melding, seeking solitude and seeking companionship to understand one's many selves. Health is seeking out all the experiences of creation and turning them over and over, feeling their texture and multiple meanings. Health is expanding beyond one's singular state of consciousness to experience the ripples and waves of the universe.
—JEANNE ACHTERBERG

Healer of Hearts

Dr. Dean Ornish's book *Love and Survival* is both a personal and professional study of the importance of love to health and happiness. Dr. Dean confided to me over dinner in San Francisco, where he lives, that he had once flirted with suicide. He'd achieved phenomenal success as a respected cardiologist and best-selling author. His medical program to reverse coronary artery disease had gained national recognition. Dean's mission is to lower the human toll of heart disease and to make an impact upon the staggering fact that bypass surgery is a $26 billion-a-year business. He was, at the time, also helping develop a program with a guy we both knew named Michael Milken (the notorious junk bond king) to prevent and treat prostate disease.

Yet Dean was absolutely miserable. He began to doubt his abilities, had a fear of failing, suffered from insomnia, exhaustion, and despair. Dean confided that inside he'd felt like a fraud. But what had depressed him the most was that none of his achievements were bringing him lasting happiness. "I was in so much pain, I could barely function," he remembered. But his saving grace now sat across the table from us. Molly, a lovely woman, taught him that love is critical to survival. As we parted that evening, Dean sighed, "I learned that when my work is ego driven, it makes me lonely. But when I approach it in the spirit of service, I'm much happier." Have you ever experienced an "Is that all there is?" letdown after an accomplishment?

Dean discovered that whenever you extend yourself, you make your life better as well as making things around you better. Service pays a psychic dividend.

Blessed is the influence of one true, loving, human soul on another.
—GEORGE ELIOT

Help Yourself As You Help Others

Service is the work of the soul. It pays psychic dividends. You feel engaged with the rest of humanity. You're taking a step toward solving some problem. You're making things better, which serves you and others well. When you reach out to others in distress, you see your own blessings more clearly. You become aware of what you've been taking for granted and what you're glad you don't have.

Research supports this notion that when we give to others, we give to ourselves. Michigan researchers who studied twenty-seven hundred people for almost ten years found that men who regularly did volunteer work had death rates two and one half times lower than men who didn't. When was the last time you performed a good deed?

Even watching others doing good boosts your immune system. College students were shown a clip of Mother Teresa performing her charitable acts of love on the filthy streets of Calcutta. Components in the college students' saliva, which had been previously tested, were found to have increased fivefold. Their IGA, immunoglobulin, was greatly stimulated simply by watching altruistic acts! You feel positive about yourself when you do for others. A Vanderbilt study showed that ego strength is the number-one predictor of whether a patient will experience an acute or chronic illness, and for how long.

Perhaps this is why some of our nation's most generous philanthropists, like John D. Rockefeller (age ninety-eight), have lived to such a ripe old age. Writing this book of support and help to you is part of my way of serving.

Psychologist Robert Ornstein and physician David Sobel are well known for their research into the health effects of doing good to others. In their book *Healthy Pleasures,* they describe what they call the "helper's high," a kind of euphoria volunteers get when helping others—a warm glow in the chest and a sense of vitality that comes from being simultaneously energized and calm. They compare it to a runner's high, and it is caused by the body's release of our favorite neurochemicals, endorphins.

And the process doesn't flow just one way. Researcher Daniel Wirth claims that studies in psychoneuroimmunology suggest that every one of us has the capacity to effect the healing of others. In other words, when we act in loving ways toward others, we are strengthening not only our own immune systems, but those of the people we help. A win-win situation.

It is in offering ourselves to the suffering, broken, and excluded of our world that we ourselves become whole. —KILLIAN NOE

Two Ears and Only One Mouth

If you are looking for a way to be of service to others, there's no easier place to start than by being a good listener, particularly if you listen with your heart as well as your ears. You'll impress someone much more with attentive silence than you can by trying to top their stories. Listening has become a lost art in this yammering society. I may be a talker, good for sixty words a minute with gusts up to eighty. (And I'm a Southerner, too. Imagine if I were from New York!) But I'm also a dedicated listener.

One of my enjoyments is being in the presence of somebody who's willing to meet me at soul level. Since our egos get addicted to self-importance, when I do meet a person who's truly present and willing to be vulnerable and transparent, and candidly disclose themselves to me, it becomes a level playing field for mutual discovery. I call it the "exquisite reality." The Greeks call it *kairos*. This is when I'm so interested in hearing your story that I literally lose track of time.

We can become "The Balm Squad" if we're comforting someone who is struggling with the same issues as we. We may confide in that person the fears and doubts we don't dare lay on a family member. We can share therapy suggestions, referrals, and recommendations. It's reassuring to realize we're not alone.

Our deepest concerns are not exclusive to us. When we feel known, we become more hopeful. Optimism is contagious. Have you experienced this?

It was the Reverend Dan Scott, one of the most significant people in my life, who showed me that listening is the oldest form of healing. The first time he came by after my diagnosis, I was so anticipating some magic words from this mighty man of God. As I lay with my eyes closed, Dan solemnly pulled up a chair beside my bed. I awaited some magnificent prayer to help me awaken from my nightmare of hepatitis C. But only silence followed. Tiny drops of water fell on the back of my hand. When I peeked with one eye, I saw Brother Dan crying. Listening can be a sacrament. Sometimes we need to meet the other person just exactly where they are. We can offer silence as our gift as we bear witness to their suffering. Who's the best listener you know?

Listening well will grant you insights into your own behavior. I know 'cause I used to be a screamer. I overcompensated because I had no partner to support me in raising the girls. Maybe if I turned up the volume and intensity I'd get through? Finally, one day Wynonna and Ashley told me that when I screamed or yelled it produced the opposite effect of what I intended. Because I was all she had, when Wy saw me lose it, it terrified her. Ash admitted that when she saw me out of control, she immediately began coming up with her alibi and her defense. She's slick as snot on a doorknob. Remember, Ashley's an actress! I learned much too late that if a parent will patiently assume a relaxed body posture and sincerely offer to listen, kids will eventually share their inner lives. They'll either hang themselves or discover more truth within themselves. The same is true for adults.

Relaxed listening moves you beyond chatter. You gather information. Others' opinions may prompt you to hold your beliefs up to the light. Listening fosters mutual respect. It reduces tension. You don't lose your voice. (If a pig loses its voice, is it disgruntled?)

With silence as their benediction, God's angels come.
When in the presence of a great affliction, the soul sits dumb.
—JOHN GREENLEAF WHITTIER

Your Turn Now

When was the last time you did something charitable that didn't involve your checkbook? Serving others doesn't have to be complicated, difficult, or costly. Here are some ways to begin:

- Catch yourself the next time you're in a conversation. Are you attentively listening, or merely waiting for your chance to speak? Do you tend to try to top the other person's story? Do you ever try to finish another's sentence? Truly listening is giving of yourself.

- Do a random act of kindness—pay someone's bridge toll; feed a stranger's parking meter; hide $10 in someone's desk to surprise them; send an anonymous letter of support to someone going through a hard time. Smile at everyone. You'll cheer up not only their day, but yours as well.

- Check out www.volunteermatch.org. It's a matching service linking people who want to volunteer with opportunities in their local communities. It has matched over a million folks so far. You can browse all the places near you that are looking for help and see if anything jumps out at you.

- If something angers or frustrates you, get involved. Having once wished for a better home for my kids, I got involved with Habitat for Humanity.

- What do you love? Share that. If you love to garden, teach a class at the community center. If you love to cook, make extra and hand it out to homeless people. Drop off for a visit at the home of an elderly neighbor or a busy mom with lots of kids. Giving doesn't have to be painful. When we give from overflow, from where generosity naturally flows in us, our giving will not deplete us.

Ultimately, what we have to give others is the fruit of the work we have done on ourselves. Dramatic life change gives us a chance to outgrow our pettiness, to step out of our past through the doorway of awareness into the light of truth of who we really are—to discover the seat of our soul and then to understand how interdependent we all are. From that knowing, we become able to offer the best of ourselves to others. Love is the glue holding this whole thing together. Milton Mayeroff called love "the selfless promotion of the growth of another." When you and I harness our individual potential to expand in love, we put an *R* in front of our own evolution. We do our part in creating a revolution to become the human family instead of the human race.

Catholic priest Henri Nouwen spoke of this truth when he wrote, "In the giving it becomes clear that we are chosen, blessed and broken not simply for our own sakes, but so that all we are about, all that we live, finds its final significance in its being lived for others."

*Our task here is to become more Godlike, to recognize
the divine and spiritual nature of our souls. To do that
we need to unlearn fear, violence, greed, ego and power.
Then kindness, joy, love and spiritual wisdom are all there.*

—BRIAN WEISS, PH.D.

Parting Thoughts

*I*t has been satisfying to be your companion as you begin this part of your journey of self-discovery. For me it's also the beginning of the fulfillment of my promise to honor your request for a series of books for your further healing. "Promise" comes from the Latin word that means "to send forth." My experiences have taught me that you and I get three educations in life. The first comes from our family of origin, the second from our schools. The third and most intriguing learning opportunity is the sum of everyday choices we make for ourselves as adults. I hope you'll reread this first book and discuss what you've learned with others.

All that happens to us, good and bad, presents great possibilities for emotional and spiritual growth. You and I have free will. We can pick and choose what will better serve our happiness. I hope the concepts here will help you gain clarity about what you want to release as you come to understand how it's no longer serving you well.

As you now know, I'm living proof that all of our difficulties can be the stepping-stones to self-actualization and fulfillment. But I'm just a messenger. Are you willing to open your eyes to see the choices that will turn your scars into stars? Pierre Teilhard de Chardin said, "The whole of life lies in the word 'seeing.' "

Ultimately any chance for personal happiness comes down to realizing that this is it. This is your one and only short and precious life. It could end at any time. This present moment is really all we have.

I was rushing to catch a plane one day, and just before I handed the gate agent my ticket, a gentleman at the next gate spied me. Dropping his carry-on bag and jacket, he rushed over. I could see in a flash that he was very ill. With tear-filled eyes, he began to tell me that he'd been following my journey. He was now headed home to break the news to his family that he was in the last stages of full-blown AIDS. Wy's and my song "Love Can Build a Bridge" was number one on the radio at the time. He'd sent the CD to his family, along with a letter preparing them.

The gate agents were beckoning to both of us. "What can you tell me?" he pleaded. It all seemed preposterous. A stranger preparing to make life's final passage seeking words of wisdom from me. In such instances, I've learned to live in the present and in God's presence. I chose to stand still and let God move.

The word "peace" tumbled out. "Peace assures you that you are loved and never alone—that everything is all right just the way it is. Fear is robbing you of enjoying your moments. It is not how many breaths you take in your lifetime that matters; it's how many moments that take your breath away. When you understand you can't experience fear and peace in the same thought, you can choose peace with every breath. Join our circle of believers who choose to walk toward the light. Take comfort in the revelation that peace of mind is the ultimate goal for all of us. All is well. All is well."

Now these are my parting words to you as you come to the end of this first book. This is really your beginning. The more you come to understand the transformative power of these twenty breakthrough choices, the more you will know peace.

Where do we grow from here . . . ?

Still in one peace,

Naomi, aka Soul Survivor
September 2003

Acknowledgments

*I*n *Modern Man in Search of a Soul* Carl Jung wrote, "The meeting of two personalities is like the contact of two chemical substances. If there is any reaction, both are transformed."

I feel gratefulness (a great fullness in my heart) to the following esteemed members of the scientific community for explaining their important research and even befriending me:

Blair Justice, Ph.D., psychologist specializing in mind-body-spirit research, whose groundbreaking book *Who Gets Sick: How Beliefs, Moods and Thoughts Affect Your Health* launched my investigation into how we can influence our own immune system. This information facilitated my own healing.

Leon Lederman, Ph.D. (aka: E=mc²), Nobel laureate in physics, for exposing me to the fascinating world of physics and the mysteries of the universe. You've opened my mind to infinite possibilities.

Andrew Weil, M.D., best-selling author and the premier pioneer in complementary medicine, for proving how integrating the best of allopathic medicine with complementary techniques does more than address symptoms but also strives to heal the whole person. I put your theory to the test and found "both are better."

Mona Lisa Schulz, M.D., Ph.D. (aka: Hummingbird), Neuropsychiatrist and Medical Intuitive who uses her own intuitive genius to demonstrate to others (like me) how to access their own inner guidance system. Our daylong and all-night kitchen table conversations on brain plasticity and functioning continue to educate, stimulate, and guide me.

Bruce R. Bacon, M.D. (aka: Dr. Right), James F. King MD Endowed Chair in Gastroenterology, professor of internal medicine, and director of the Division of Gastroenterology and Hepatology at the St. Louis University School of Medicine, one of the most important leaders in the battle to treat and find a cure for hepatitis C. I had to kiss a few frogs till I met you.

Francis Collins, M.D., Ph.D. (aka: "The Lifeguard of the Human Genome Pool"), director of the Human Genome Research Project at the NIH, decoder of the human genome sequence, and ethical visionary in genomic predictability. Thanks for helping me understand the role heredity plays in causing and predicting disease. Our conversations of nature versus nurture have been enormously enlightening!

Dean Ornish, M.D., cardiologist and best-selling author. I greatly appreciate the manner in which you use your academic credibility as well as your personal experience to substantiate the role good diet, a support system, and connectedness play in our health and even longevity.

Christiane Northrup, M.D., for tireless promotion of women's health issues, especially the understanding of menopause. I continue to benefit from your knowledge of how emotions and spirituality influence all stages of the feminine life cycle.

Dr. Mel Elson, for facilitating my zeal to empower women through encouraging them to be defined from within and thereby looking better on the outside. Collaborating on our skincare line, "ESTEEM by Naomi Judd," has given me a vehicle to promote my philosophy and fulfill my purpose.

Joan Borysenko, Ph.D., cancer cell biologist, clinical psychologist, author, lecturer, and one of the most inspiring and knowledgeable voices for holistic approaches to healing soma, psyche, and spirit. Your work on the benefits of forgiveness has been so freeing for me.

Alan Brownstein and the American Liver Foundation, tireless warriors on behalf of the 40 million sufferers of hepatitis C and the 25 million who have other forms of liver disease.

Frank Sulloway, Ph.D., psychologist at Stanford University, who has discovered the role birth order plays in personality development and sociability. Your findings help me understand why my family members and I think and act the way we do.

Kary Mullis, Ph.D. and Nobel laureate in chemistry, inventor of DNA cloning and the polymerase chain reaction. Thanks for educating me on how to interpret my lab values, especially the viral load by PCR.

Rachel Naomi Remen, M.D., (aka: "wounded healer"), the cofounder of Commonweal Cancer Retreat. I stand in awe of your compassion, insight, and personal courage in healing. I agree that our health care system itself is sick and needs help. You motivate me to do my part.

Marvin Minsky, Ph.D., one of the founding fathers of artificial intelligence at MIT, who encourages and goads me to think out of the box and question everything. You make my brain cells vibrate at a high frequency.

Candace Pert, Ph.D., iconoclastic neuropharmacologist and biophysicist researcher, who discovered the opiate receptors and helped identify neuropeptides, the biochemical equivalents of our thoughts and feelings. Awareness of these "molecules of emotions" has been instrumental in prompting me to choose positivism, thereby stimulating my immune system.

Larry Dossey, M.D., whose documentation of how prayer works has given scientific credibility to the beneficial role faith plays in healing, wellness, and happiness. Your belief that we are spiritual beings having a human experience helped me deal with my body's failings.

Caroline Myss, Ph.D., thought-provoking instructor on the anatomy of our spirits and on why some people prevent themselves from healing, the role of archetypes, and how to find life purpose. You reminded me not to become a wound addict.

Judith Orloff, M.D., psychiatrist, who shows us how to start paying attention to the invisible world by tapping into our intuition. She reminded me that our voyage of self-discovery begins not in the world outside but within us.

Joel Hargrove, M.D., consummate country doctor, who is also on the cutting edge of bioidentical hormone replacement therapy. My husband and children thank you too.

Steven Pinker, Ph.D., professor of psychology and director of the Center for Cognitive Neuroscience at MIT. Our conversations on the seat of conscience, language, and how emotionality drives all behavior have been stimulating and instrumental in my self-repair process.

Steve Rosenberg, M.D., chief of surgery at the National Cancer Institute. Indomitable crusader for cancer research and treatment who set the example of the way doctors should align themselves as partners with their patients on their healing journey.

Elaine and Joe Sullivan, whose own marriage and family life speak as eloquently as their decades of healing work. Thank you for showing the power of stories and guided imagery as valuable resources in resolving past trauma and bringing about peace of mind.

Ben Carson, M.D., chief of pediatric neurosurgery at Johns Hopkins, whose skilled hands are matched by his caring, empathic demeanor and his personal triumph over adversity. I agree that we must combine the art of healing with the science of medical technology to treat the whole person.

Gladys McGarey, M.D., first president of the American Holistic Physicians Association. A medical feminist who was integrative when integrative wasn't cool. It's your shoulders I'm standing on.

Senate Majority Leader and cardiologist Dr. Bill Frist, who's showing me how to work within the political system for various aspects of health care reform. You're muy sympatico in getting "managed care" to manage to care and putting compassion and common sense into health care (versus wealth care).

Mehmet Oz, M.D. (aka: Dr. Big Heart), cardiovascular surgeon at Columbia Presbyterian Hospital, who addresses his patients' emotional concerns and promotes stress reduction before, during, and after operating. Thanks for being one of the most vocal and visible faces of complementary medicine.

Marianne Williamson, visionary, who eloquently uses parables and paints metaphors to report on the state of the collective soul, rekindle community building, and spur a revolution in responsible politics.

Brian Luke Seaward, Ph.D., recognized authority on the detrimental role of stress on our biopsychospiritual health. I'm indebted to you for teaching that 75 percent of our illnesses are stress related. You are my favorite resource on relaxation and the practice of mindfulness.

Dr. Elisabeth Kübler-Ross, whose landmark theories on death and dying guide and comfort us through the universal stages of grieving. Thanks for proving that talking about death won't kill us.

Bill Phillips, Ph.D., Nobel laureate in physics, whom I thank for sharing his genius about the structure of the universe and how it works to substantiate the existence of God. Science explains how, but spirituality tells us why. I agree with you that we can build a bridge between science and spirituality.

Belongingness by Blood and Marriage: Larry, Ashley and Dario, Wynonna and Roach, Elijah and Grace and Zack, Mom, Polly Judd, sis Margaret Mandell and family, brother Rev. Mark Judd and family, and my dear aunts and uncles.

The Ladies of The Round Table: Dorthey Newcome, Dena DiVito, Nancye Green, Kathy Allman, Mary Jane Ryan, Marina Torpin, Linda Stone.

Spiritual mentors: the Reverend Dan Scott, and Don and Christine Potter. Thanks for keeping me aware that our problems are spiritual and therefore have spiritual solutions.

The Bookends: Amanda Murray, my editor, and Mel Berger, the world's finest literary agent and one funny stand-up comedian.

Plato wrote: Paying attention and truly looking and listening are a form of love.

My appreciation to all you folks I've met in my travels who've contributed to this book by expressing your feelings and telling me your stories. These pages are the result of my looking and listening and paying attention.

Index